Horatio McCulloch 1805-1867

Sheenah Smith

Glasgow Museums and Art Galleries

Subsidised by the Scottish Arts Council

HORATIO McCULLOCH EXHIBITION 1988

Glasgow Art Gallery and Museum
  6 May — 26 June

Dundee Art Gallery and Museum
  9 July — 27 August

Aberdeen Art Gallery and Museum
  10 September — 1 October

Nottingham University Art Gallery
  11 October — 12 November

The Fine Art Society, London
  21 November — 16 December

Cover illustration Cat No 46

Published by Glasgow Museums and Art Galleries

Designed by Judith Wilder

Photographs of works in Glasgow Art Gallery collection
and those loaned from private collections, by Glasgow
Museums Photographic Department

© 1988 Glasgow Museums and Art Galleries

ISBN 0 902752 35 9

CONTENTS

ACKNOWLEDGEMENTS

Many people have participated in the production of this catalogue but I would like to thank especially those who contributed as volunteers in the Fine Art Department. The first to be
directly involved was Nancy Brown Colvin, a graduate in Fine
Arts of the University of Pittsburgh. Nancy carried out a great
deal of preliminary research and was particularly adept at root-
ing out elusive manuscript material. Her work helped to provide the basis from which the project was developed. More recently Tarn Brown, Teresa Lowe, Gaynor Macfarlane and above
all Janice Slater have retrieved an enormous amount of information from such sources as contemporary newspapers and
street directories. Their many hours spent in libraries have resulted in a more comprehensive account of the artist and his
work than would otherwise have been possible. Other volunteers who have helped with historical research include Ann
Barlow, Belinda Barnett, Jacqueline van Bavel, Julie Biggs,
Janice Chalmers, Susan Heys, Marianne Gilchrist, Claire Plumb,
Claire Spence and Lisa Stapleton.

The many friends and colleagues who have assisted with in-
formation and advice include Valerie Boa, Patrick Bourne, Meg
Buchanan, Michael Donnelly, Lindsay Errington, Alison Fergu-
son, Martin Forrest, Ian Gow, Andrew Greg, Martin Hopkinson,
John Harrower, James Holloway, Francina Irwin, Elspeth King,
Duncan Macmillan, Andrew McIntosh Patrick, Robin Rodger,
David Scruton, Meta Viles, Isobel Walker and Eunice Wright.
Others who have contributed specific pieces of information are
acknowledged in the relevant parts of the text.

Norma Johnson and Joyce Townsend, as well as compiling
the technical report published on p 103, were unfailingly
patient and helpful when their advice was sought on matters of
technique and authenticity.

The author is particularly grateful to Anne Donald, Marjorie
Allthorpe Guyton and Patricia Bascom for valuable comments,
suggestions and editorial advice. Special thanks are also due to
Martha Campbell for expertly transforming a jumbled draft
into an orderly typescript. The good-humoured co-operation
of colleagues in the photography and design departments,
despite many other pressures, was greatly appreciated.

FOREWORD

Horatio McCulloch, Scotland's most popular Victorian landscape painter is known today for a handful of famous images such as *Glencoe, Loch Katrine* and *Loch Lomond.*

Glasgow Art Gallery has the largest collection of his work and it seemed appropriate for this institution to organise the present exhibition which was planned to coincide with the celebrations of Mayfest and Glasgow's Garden Festival. The selection has been made around a core of sixteen pictures already in Glasgow's collection, the majority of which date from McCulloch's last two decades and are the kind of exhibition pieces which brought him success during his lifetime. His early works, watercolours and oil sketches have not been grouped together since 1867 when the only previous exhibition of McCulloch's work was shown in Edinburgh a few months after his death.

The present exhibition, like that one, aims to present a coherent picture of McCulloch's range and development as an artist, within the limits imposed by financial restrictions and by present knowledge of the whereabouts of his work. The organisers have been extremely fortunate in receiving enthusiastic response from owners of paintings (listed on p 111). We would particularly like to thank the private lenders, many of whom in the first instance drew attention to the works in their possession, who allowed repeated invasions of their homes and in several cases consented to their pictures being away for a year or longer. Special mention must be made of two expatriate Scots, one from Canada and the other from the south coast of England, who personally arranged the delivery of their loans to Glasgow.

The co-operation of colleagues in other museums and galleries is greatly appreciated. Several have taken a great deal of trouble to prepare exhibits specially for this exhibition and, condition permitting, all loan requests have been granted for both the Glasgow showing and the tour.

We owe a special debt of gratitude to The Paul Mellon Centre for Studies in British Art whose financial support allowed all appropriate items to be fully illustrated in colour in the catalogue, and to The Scottish Arts Council who generously subsidised the Exhibition.

My particular thanks go to Sheenah Smith, Depute Keeper of Fine Art, for bringing to our attention, and for our appreciation, the work of this fine and largely underrated landscape painter.

Alasdair A Auld
DIRECTOR

BIBLIOGRAPHICAL ABBREVIATIONS

Brydall	Robert Brydall *Art in Scotland, its origin and progress* Edinburgh and London 1889
Caw	James L Caw *Scottish Painting Past and Present 1620-1908* Edinburgh 1908
Chambers	Robert Chambers *A Biographical Dictionary of Eminent Scotsmen* revised edition, edited by Rev Thomas Thomson London 1870
Cursiter	Stanley Cursiter *Scottish Art* London 1949
Donnelly	Gerald Donnelly *John Knox a Transitional Figure and The Picturesque Tour in Scotland* 1987 (Glasgow University unpublished History of Art Honours Dissertation)
DNB	Dictionary of National Biography
Fraser	Alexander Fraser *Scottish Landscape The works of Horatio Macculloch RSA* Edinburgh 1872
Halsby	Julian Halsby *Scottish Watercolours 1740-1940* London 1986
100 Glasgow Men	*Memoirs and Portraits of 100 Glasgow Men* 2 vols 1886
Irwin	David and Francina Irwin *Scottish Painters at Home and Abroad 1700-1900* London 1985
1974 Knox Exh	Glasgow Art Gallery and Museum *John Knox Landscape Painter* (Ian McClure) Exh Cat 1974
McKay	William D McKay *The Scottish School of Painting* London 1906
RAPFAS *Reports*	Annual *Reports* of the Royal Association for the Promotion of the Fine Arts in Scotland 1834-69. (Some copies in NLS, Mitchell Library and GUL, no complete run located)
Rinder & McKay	Frank Rinder and W D McKay *The Royal Scottish Academy 1826-1916* Glasgow 1917
Watson *Catalogue*	W F Watson *Edinburgh: its Houses and its noted Inhabitants . . .* Architectural Institute of Scotland Edinburgh 1865

SELECTED ABBREVIATIONS

APFAS	Association for the Promotion of the Fine Arts in Scotland
BM	British Museum
DS	Dilettanti Society
EUL	Edinburgh University Library
GAG	Glasgow Art Gallery
GIFA	Glasgow Institute of the Fine Arts
GUA	Glasgow University Archives
GUL	Glasgow University Library
NGS	National Gallery of Scotland
NLS	National Library of Scotland
NRH	New Register House, Edinburgh
OWCS	Old Water Colour Society
RA	Royal Academy
RSA	Royal Scottish Academy
RAPFAS	Royal Association for the Promotion of the Fine Arts in Scotland
RSAMD	Royal Scottish Academy of Music and Drama
RSM	Royal Scottish Museum
SA	Scottish Academy
SNPG	Scottish National Portrait Gallery
SRA	Strathclyde Regional Archives
SRO	Scottish Record Office
SUA	Strathclyde University Archives
V & A	Victoria and Albert Museum
WSA	West of Scotland Academy

See also BIBLIOGRAPHICAL ABBREVIATIONS and list of EXHIBITED WORKS 1828-68.

PRINCIPAL CONTEMPORARY SOURCES

Published: Apart from Alexander Fraser's monograph listed above, the most productive 19th century sources have been newspapers and journals. Despite generous assistance from several of the people named on p 4, time has not allowed an exhaustive search of all available material. The following have been consulted.

> *The Art Journal*
> *The Art Union*
> *The Bailie*
> *Caledonian Mercury*
> *Edinburgh Evening Courant*
> *Edinburgh Mercury*
> *Glasgow Chronicle*
> *Glasgow Courier*
> *Glasgow Herald*
> *Glasgow Sentinel*
> *Scotsman*

Several of the above carry obituary notices containing biographical information. The most detailed are in the *Glasgow Herald* (26 June 1867), *Scotsman* (25 June 1867) and *The Art Journal* (1 Aug 1867).

Other important printed documents include the catalogue of the McCulloch Sale, Chapman's, Edinburgh 28, 29, 30 Nov and 2, 3, 7, 9, 10 Dec 1867 (annotated copy V & A Library (23D)) and the catalogue of the Nov 1867 Clark Exhibition the full title of which is *Exhibition of a selection of the Works of the late Horatio McCulloch Esq RSA in Mr Clark's Fine Art Gallery 67 Princes Street, Edinburgh 1867.* A short introduction by W D Clark is followed by a list of 82 oil paintings, nine watercolours and three portraits of the artist, together with the names of the lenders to the exhibition.

Manuscript: The majority of surviving letters from McCulloch to his friends, patrons and dealers are located in the RSA Library and in the National Library of Scotland. A few letters are held by other repositories. Individual references are given as they occur in the catalogue.

The RSA Library also contains McCulloch's Account Book (see p 22) and miscellaneous relevant material relating to the proceedings of the Academy.

David Octavius Hill 1802-70 and Robert Adamson 1821-48 HORATIO McCULLOCH *c*1845, calotype
Scottish National Portrait Gallery

EARLY YEARS IN GLASGOW
AND THE WEST OF SCOTLAND 1805-37

In the early 19th century Glasgow was a city of thriving
commerce, expanding industry and exploding popula-
tion but as an environment for the young artist it had
little to offer. There was no publicly funded art school,
no strong tradition of patronage and no regular exhibitions of modern art until 1828. Nevertheless Glasgow
was the early home of Scotland's most celebrated Victorian landscape painter, Horatio McCulloch[1].

By 1805, the year of his birth, textile manufacture was
Glasgow's leading industry and McCulloch's father, Alexander, was one of those who prospered as a result of the
cotton boom. He and his wife, Margaret Watson, had
settled in the east end of the city by the time their son
was born and named after the hero of the day, Horatio
Nelson. Although no contemporary record has been
found, later sources indicate that McCulloch was
born in November 1805 in a house at the corner of
Claythorn Street and Gallowgate[2].

In 1812 or 13 when the McCulloch family moved to a
more opulent address, 29 St Andrew's Square, a younger
child Elizabeth was about three years old and Alexander
was in business as McCulloch, Davidson & Co, manufac-
turers, trading from 15 St Andrew's Square[3]. Near neigh-
bours were the Thomson family, founders of the Adelphi
cotton works, Hutchesontown, and first owners of
Camphill House. The Thomsons were to be among the
first to buy paintings from McCulloch in the 1830s at the
start of his career as a professional artist (eg Cat No 12).

McCulloch's biographers are vague about his artistic
education. It is generally agreed that he showed an early
interest in art which was not discouraged by his family,
and that he studied under the Glasgow landscape
painter John Knox (1778-1845). However the exact date
and duration of his attachment to Knox is uncertain and
it was possibly preceded by a period of instruction from
Alexander Watt[4], another of several Glasgow drawing
teachers, or perhaps by an apprenticeship to a decorative painter. Comparison of McCulloch's technique
with that of Knox, as revealed by scientific analysis,
shows no close similarity (see technical report, p 103).

McCulloch's initial enthusiasm for art may have derived from childhood experiences. He would certainly
have seen the illuminated transparencies which at the
time were on public display whenever a notable event,
such as the King's birthday or a victory at sea, occasioned
universal celebration. A transparency was essentially a
translucent screen, often set up in a window, lit from
behind, upon which was painted an appropriate design.
Like scene painting for the theatre, the creation of

John Knox NORTH WESTERN VIEW FROM BEN LOMOND ?1834

transparencies provided welcome employment for artists throughout Britain. McCulloch himself was engaged in work of this kind as a young man (see p 16).

More exciting still for the little boy would have been a visit to one of John Knox's landscape or cityscape panoramas. Invented by Robert Barker (1739-1806) and first seen in Edinburgh in 1788, these vast painted views were in great demand in Glasgow in the early years of the 19th century. In 1810 Knox presented his 'Grand panoramic painting of the view from the top of Ben Lomond'[5], a sight which would surely have enchanted any child, but particularly one who was destined to devote his life to painting the scenery of Scotland.

The success of the Panoramas reinforced Knox's reputation as a landscape painter and art teacher[6]. As a painter he was chiefly known for his meticulously executed landscape views in the classical tradition and for busy Glasgow cityscapes. As a teacher he would have instructed his pupils in traditional methods at the same time encouraging an interest in atmospheric effects based on direct observation of nature. Whilst the extent of McCulloch's instruction under Knox is uncertain, one of his pupils from about 1819-23 was Daniel Macnee (1806-82) who later became a distinguished portrait painter, and was McCulloch's lifelong friend. The two artists first met during these adolescent years and became friends with other aspiring Glasgow artists, notably William Leighton Leitch (1804-83).

Although there were no regular exhibitions of modern art in Glasgow, McCulloch and Macnee had other opportunities for study. The old Theatre Royal (destroyed by

fire in 1829) possessed a stunning collection of scenery by the eminent Edinburgh landscape painter, Alexander Nasmyth (1758-1840), and David Roberts (1796-1864) was employed there as a scene painter in 1819-20[7]. The latter's brief stay allowed the students to see the broad effects produced by Roberts[8] and also gave them the opportunity to contrast his work with the more detailed manner of Nasmyth and of their own master, John Knox.

The University's small but choice collection of Old Master and British paintings was on show to the public at the Hunterian Museum, and the boys could also have viewed works of art in picture dealers' shops and in public auction rooms. They may have had access as well to the collections of local connoisseurs. John Strang, writing in 1830[9] names several local collectors of Old Masters singling out James Ewing, a Glasgow merchant, 'whose courteousness in admitting amateurs to view his gallery is quite proverbial'.

In 1821 the McCulloch family moved to Portland Street, Laurieston, in the Gorbals, then an elegant district, on the south side of the river. In the same year an exhibition sponsored by the Glasgow Institution for Promoting and Encouraging the Fine Arts in the West of Scotland opened on 6th August at the Gallery of Alexander Finlay, carver and gilder. There was a second exhibition of 'the works of living artists' the following year and catalogues for both shows have survived. The absence of McCulloch's name from the list of contributors may be significant because Macnee, the younger of the two boys, had work accepted for both exhibitions as did other pupils of John Knox, all exhibiting from their master's address, 40

John Knox SOUTH WESTERN VIEW FROM BEN LOMOND ?1834

Dunlop Street. The explanation is probably that McCulloch was not attached to Knox until later (and therefore not for very long) and that he had not yet developed as an easel painter. He presumably visited the exhibitions and would have seen numerous landscapes by Knox as well as the work of future Edinburgh friends such as D O Hill, Kenneth McLeay and J F Williams.

There were no further Glasgow exhibitions until 1828. Around 1824 McCulloch and Macnee left home to seek employment first briefly as snuff-box decorators with Messrs Smith at Cumnock, Ayrshire, and subsequently and more importantly with William Home Lizars (1788-1859), the Edinburgh engraver.

Lizars had studied at the Trustees Academy Edinburgh along with David Wilkie, but more or less had to abandon his career as a painter when his father died in 1812. As the eldest child it was his duty to take over his late father's engraving business in order to support his widowed mother and her large family. During the mid 1820s when Macnee and McCulloch were employed colouring prints in his workshop, Lizars was involved in the production of engraved plates for a wide variety of publications. The two young artists from Glasgow were set to work adding watercolour washes to the plates for anatomical books by their employer's brother, Dr John Lizars, and for P J Selby's *Ornithology*.

Fraser relates that McCulloch spent much of his spare time sketching around Edinburgh, but that he also found time for conviviality 'and was very popular among his companions for his good-heartedness and merry harem-scarum disposition'. One of his friends amongst the older generation was the landscape painter John Francis Williams (1785-1846) whom Fraser claims was with McCulloch during a visit to Scotland's then most admired landscape artist, Rev John Thomson of Duddingston (1778-1840). The date of their first meeting is not recorded, but McCulloch certainly had opportunities to see Thomson's work during these early years in Edinburgh, and later on he became a frequent visitor to Duddingston Manse[10].

Thomson's romantic vision of Scotland, expressed in exuberant brushwork, was a major influence in McCulloch's move away from the classical compositions and meticulous technique favoured by Nasmyth and Knox. It was probably Thomson, a friend of Sir Walter Scott and of J M W Turner, who stimulated McCulloch's awareness of the historical associations in landscape. (Titles which include phrases such as 'near the battleground of Drumclog' and 'Stronghold of the Wolf of Badenoch' are evidence of this.)

Another crucial influence from this first Edinburgh period was that of Thomson's friend the watercolour painter Hugh W Williams (1773-1829). Williams had returned in 1819 after two years in Italy and Greece bringing with him a mass of sketches which he developed as a series of large finished watercolours. These were greatly admired when exhibited in Edinburgh in 1822 and earned Williams the nickname 'Grecian'. McCulloch had access to the Greek watercolours through his employer W H Lizars and through another engraver, William Forrest (1805-89), who was later to be responsible for most of the popular engravings after

H W Williams ATHENS FROM THE EAST *c*1822

McCulloch (eg Cat Nos 32, 34). Lizars and Forrest were amongst several artists engaged in engraving H W Williams' work for publication and McCulloch's biographers tell us that the young painter was allowed to make copies of the watercolours whilst they were with the engravers. The debt to Williams is apparent in some of McCulloch's drawings of the 1830s (eg Cat No 8) whilst his later watercolours seem to owe something also to David Roberts (eg Cat No 24).

In about 1827 MCulloch's father died and Horatio returned to Glasgow. The last entry for Alexander is in the 1827 *Post Office Glasgow Directory* 'Alexander McCulloch manufacturer . . . house 3 Portland St Laurieston'. It was at this address that McCulloch rejoined his mother and sister in his new role as head of the household.

In September 1828 the first *West of Scotland exhibition of the works of living artists* opened in Glasgow's recently completed Argyll Arcade under the patronage of the Glasgow Dilettanti Society[11]. This time Horatio

McCulloch is represented, by four works, two of which he calls 'Study from Nature'. In the following year his one exhibit is a 'sketch' and in 1830 this tendency to show sketches is condemned by John Strang[12], author of the first serious criticism of the Glasgow artists' contributions to these annual exhibitions. Under the pseudonym Geoffrey Crayon, Strang published a pamphlet[9] in which an outline of the history of the Dilettanti Society and a brief survey of its first two exhibitions is followed by a detailed review of the 1830 show[13]. Of McCulloch he has this to say:

'There are four pictures, or rather one picture and three sketches, by Mr M'CULLOCH. Does this gentleman wish to hide his talents under a bushel, by sending so many sketches; or does he conceive that they are sufficiently finished for those who are likely to look at them? . . . The finished picture, No 138, [*View on Loch Lomond*] is, however, a very promising production for a young Artist. It is a well chosen point of view, the general effect is good, and the colour approaches to splendour,

Rev John Thomson GLEN OF ALTNARIE 1832

save in a few points of the extreme and middle distances, which are left in too positive patches. Were these faults amended, and the finishing, which is indispensable, attended to, we think Mr M'Culloch destined to become even a more respectable Artist, than he is now a clever sketcher.'

This criticism is understandable. To the majority of the exhibition-going public of the day, McCulloch's work of this period must have seemed unacceptably slap-dash, and in any case sketches were not yet considered suitable for public exhibition. Other more eminent artists than he had been similarly attacked for lack of finish (eg Constable, Turner, Rev Thomson). The few of McCulloch's paintings of the early 1830s which have been located so far reveal that he had already discarded the notion of elaborate finish and was painting in a fluid manner, influenced by Rev Thomson but based on direct observation of nature. In composition too he often disregarded tradition by presenting open-ended designs which are closer to the actual appearance of a landscape (eg Cat No 3) than to the Italianate views of Nasmyth and Knox.

Strang concludes his review of the 1830 exhibition by expressing regret at the lack of patrons amongst the Glasgow merchants. McCulloch and Macnee, however, had found a benefactor in James Lumsden (1778-1856) Glasgow stationer and publisher, and a friend of John Strang. One of Macnee's 1830 Dilettanti Society exhibits was a portrait of Lumsden whilst the one subject of McCulloch's which was highly commended by Strang, *View on Loch Lomond*, was engraved for a new edition of Lumsden's *Steam-Boat Companion* (which was published in August 1831 with text by Strang). The task of providing illustrations for this guidebook was shared by McCulloch and an Edinburgh artist, J B Kidd (1808-89), the latter presumably undertaking the Edinburgh subjects whilst McCulloch contributed the Glasgow and West of Scotland views[14]. Another of his 1830 titles, *High Church, Glasgow, from Duke-Street* was also used to illustrate a guidebook (see Cat No 1) and these early commissions were soon followed by further orders for topographical views from book and print publishers. McCulloch's employment as an illustrator to William Beattie's *Scotland* (London, 1838) alongside the well-established topographical artists Thomas Allom (1804-72) and W H Bartlett (1809-54) was something of an honour and of great value as a means of circulating his work amongst a wider audience. Although he is represented by only four plates, his name is on the title page with Allom and Bartlett who between them supplied over 100 illustrations (an additional three plates were after G Campion and one was after W Purser).

LOCH LOMOND engraving after McCulloch in *Lumsden's Steam-Boat Companion* 1831

SCENE IN CADZOW PARK   Engraving after McCulloch in Beattie's *Scotland* 1838

These few commissions and occasional picture sales[15] were not enough to provide a steady income. Although Lumsden reputedly helped his young protégé on more than one occasion, financing a sketching trip to the Trossachs[16], and more importantly, employing him to 'paint some large pictures for a public hall he had just built in St George's Place' (see entry for Cat No 16), other sources of finance were necessary. For this McCulloch continued to execute decorative work: landscape panels for steamship interiors[17], patriotic transparencies, and, according to Fraser, scene painting for provincial theatres.

His regular contributions to the annual exhibitions in both Glasgow and Edinburgh reveal that as yet McCulloch restricted his sketching trips to the west of Scotland, with visits to the islands of Bute and Arran providing a new range of subject matter in 1831 and 1833 respectively. The small freely-painted oil sketches which

McCulloch brought back from these expeditions (Cat Nos 5, 6) derive from Knox. The latter artist was never criticised for exhibiting sketches, but a group of small studies (some of which were included in the 1974 Knox Exh) prove that he painted out of doors in a spontaneous manner quite unlike his exhibition style.

In 1832 the Dilettanti Society held its exhibition in new rooms, in Buchanan Street, McCulloch sold two pictures and was on the Committee of the Society for the first time. He is listed as an artist-member together with Andrew Donaldson (1790-1846), drawing teacher and watercolour painter, and John D Gibson (?-1852), portrait painter. Lay members included Archibald McLellan (1797-1854) whose collection of Old Master paintings forms the core of the present Glasgow Art Gallery collection. The exhibition that year passed virtually unnoticed in the local press, where far more momentous events took precedence — the cholera epidemic, the death of Sir Walter Scott and the first election after the passing of the Reform Bill.

In 1833 however the *Courier* critic wrote enthusiastically about 'the "treasures rich and rare" with which the walls are gorgeously adorned' and lamented the lack of interest shown by the public at large. His review noted '. . . a marked improvement in the pictures of various of our Glasgow artists, and in none more so than in those of our young friend, M'Culloch, some of whose attractive and boldly designed landscapes have already met with purchasers . . . M'Culloch has a noble conception of the sublime and magnificent; and his colouring is always managed with admirable effect'.

McCulloch's passions for music, painting and poetry were nurtured during these youthful Glasgow days. He and Macnee were amongst a group of Glasgow artists, writers and musicians who congregated at the home of William Thomson (*c*1777-1853) of Kirkintilloch in the 1830s[18], and there were many contacts as well with the Edinburgh art world. McCulloch and several of his Glasgow contemporaries exhibited regularly with the Scottish Academy (later RSA) and when the 'Association for the Promotion of the Fine Arts in Scotland' (APFAS) came into being in 1834, its Edinburgh-based committee invited Archibald McLellan to represent Glasgow. As its name proclaims, APFAS aimed to promote art in Scotland. It did this through purchasing works from the Scottish Academy exhibitions and distributing them as prizes in an annual lottery open to all subscribers. It is not a surprise to find McCulloch's *View in Cadzow Park* listed as third prize in 1835, for he had already made a name for himself in the capital — in 1834 his work had been well received by Edinburgh critics: 'This artist is destined to be at the head of his profession as a landscape painter'[19]

and he was elected Associate of the Scottish Academy towards the end of that year[20].

The Edinburgh critics again praised McCulloch's exhibits in 1835 (see Cat Nos 12, 13) and D O Hill in a letter to Lord Cockburn had this to say in connection with the Glasgow Dilettanti Society '. . . There are few artists resident in the West of Scotland who are members the only two who are distinguished are messrs Graham and McCulloch . . .'[21]

Hill was not alone in dismissing the majority of Glasgow artists. Later that year, admirers of McCulloch enraged the Glasgow art establishment by publishing a blatantly partial review of that year's Dilettanti Society Exhibition. Instead of the customary fairly bland newspaper comments, an inflammatory pamphlet was issued entitled *A Glance at the Glasgow Dilettanti Society's Exhibition*[22], in which exaggerated praise for McCulloch and for his friends John Sheriff (1816-44) and Robert Maxwell (see entry for No 2) is accompanied by condemnation of other Glasgow artists, in particular Andrew Donaldson.

It was quickly followed by a second pamphlet[23] in which two authors challenge the contents of *A Glance*. The first writer attempts to smooth things over by drawing attention to McCulloch's good points whilst absolving him from responsibility for the outrageous eulogy compiled by his admirers: 'Mr M'Culloch is a young artist of great promise. We are sorry, indeed, that his friends have been so injudicious as to throw him, and his pictures in the faces of all the other exhibitors'. This respondent suggests that these admirers are McCulloch's artist-friends, and castigates them for ungentlemanly behaviour towards Donaldson. Of McCulloch he continues 'He sketches with great truth and spirit and handles his pencil [brush] after a fashion that we could almost envy. He has an excellent perception of the beautiful effects of nature, and these he transfers to his canvas with great freedom, and, at the same time, with fidelity.' Even so, of the picture at the centre of the controversy, McCulloch's exhibit *A waterfall in the Rooking Glen*[24], the same writer comments that 'it is a mere trifle, of which Mr M'Culloch, after all he has heard about it, must, by this time, be most ashamed'. Unfortunately this picture is now untraced so it is not possible to judge the degree of prejudice of the respective writers.

The second contributor to this publication is less restrained. His argument takes the form of a highly emotional letter (signed Peter Pindar, jun), in which he quotes extensively from the now lost first pamphlet[25] and sets out to demonstrate that it is 'a piece of heartless malignity', insisting that the excessive praise of McCulloch is unwarranted: 'Mr M'Culloch is as yet a very ordinary artist, and he is in a fair way to become worse'. The next sentence adds a little to our fragmented knowledge of McCulloch's early career: 'Indeed, his very good friends . . . seem afraid that he shall degenerate into a mere house painter. This would be nothing to be lamented, for better men than he have been house painters. . . . It is not very handsome of M'Culloch to turn his back upon the painting of of steam boat panels — a branch of the profession which he but lately followed; . . .'. The writer then goes on to demolish McCulloch's artist friends Robert Maxwell and John Sheriff concluding '. . . The first [McCulloch] has considerable talent, the second has a small quantity, and the third has absolutely none at all. The first was lately a painter of window screens for illumination nights . . .' — again adding important contemporary evidence to later biographers' accounts of McCulloch's early career. However the writer's intention was not to provide future historians with interesting facts, it was to deflate the three young artists and to challenge the adulation expressed in *A Glance*. Whether or not he had a hand in the writing of the pamphlet there is plenty of evidence that Professor John Wilson (1785-1854) alias 'Christopher North' admired McCulloch[26], in fact 'Peter Pindar' draws attention to Wilson's patronage of the young artist by saying 'It is very clear that he [McCulloch] will never be what is called a great artist even although Professor Wilson should take him by the hand.' Wilson himself has left proof of his respect for the artist. In an essay entitled 'Our Parish'[27] he remembers the village of Mearns (about ten miles south-west of Glasgow) where he was at school in the 1790s '. . . M'Culloch, the great Glasgow painter — and in Scotland he has no superior — will perhaps accompany you to what was once the Moor'. Christopher North laments the destruction of the Parish as he knew it and is gratified that McCulloch '. . . has shown it more than once on bits of canvas not a foot long . . .'[28]. McCulloch's obituary in *The Art Journal* draws attention to their friendship.

McCulloch would almost certainly have been aware of Professor Wilson during his first period in Edinburgh in the mid 1820s and may have made his acquaintance then. This was Wilson's heyday as the newly appointed and wildly popular Professor of Moral Philosophy and as writer for *Blackwoods Edinburgh Magazine*. He was a cult figure, especially amongst his students and other young people. It may be more than coincidence that McCulloch's early heroes, Rev Thomson of Duddingston and H W Williams, were singled out by Wilson as Scotland's best landscape painters and that McCulloch's admiration for Wordsworth was also shared by the Professor.

Daniel McNee HORATIO McCULLOCH 1828 (Cat No 62)

Whoever were the authors, the 1835 pamphlets must have caused some distress and embarrassment to McCulloch. He severed all contact with the Dilettanti Society and moved away from his native city to Hamilton, a prosperous town to the south of Glasgow made famous by its proximity to the grandiose Palace of the Dukes of Hamilton. McCulloch had already made sketching trips in the neighbourhood and his choice of home was no doubt influenced by the fact that Cadzow Forest would now be only a short distance from his door whilst Bothwell Castle and other favourite Clyde Valley subjects were not far away. Fraser (p 31) hints that a romance with the daughter of Lord Douglas' librarian attracted McCulloch to Bothwell, but nothing more is known of this episode.

The house which Horatio shared with his mother and his sister Elizabeth was Allan Bank[29] a detached villa to the south of the town. Although McCulloch is the only artist listed as resident in Hamilton in 1837[30] he was near enough to Glasgow for frequent contact with old

LOCH-AN-EILIN engraving after McCulloch 1839

friends. In June 1836 Dr Robert Macnish (1802-37) and Daniel Macnee joined him for a visit to nearby Hamilton Palace[31] a part of which was open to the public each summer[32]. As well as the family portraits and the famous Rubens *Daniel in the Lion's Den*, visitors are thought to have been allowed access to the series of Old State Rooms which contained the spectacular collection of Old Master paintings[33]. McCulloch would have seen landscapes by Salvator Rosa, Castiglione and Nicolas Poussin as well as several by 17th century Dutch masters including Hobbema, Van der Neer and Wouvermans. Of the British school there was little to be seen. It is unlikely that Gainsborough's *Wooded River Landscape*[34] was on public display and Richard Wilson's *Rome and the Ponte Molle*[35] which could convincingly be put forward as the inspiration for McCulloch's 1837 oil *Bothwell Castle* (Cat No 15) is not recorded at Hamilton Palace until much later. Further visits by McCulloch are recorded in the Visitor's Book[36], on 9 June and 15 July 1837 and on 5 May 1838, just before he left to set up house in Edinburgh.

According to Fraser, during his Hamilton years McCulloch was encouraged by Lady Belhaven of Wishaw House who acquired his study for the large oil, *Loch-an-Eilin* (described below) and by her sister, Lady Ruthven of Barncluith. Amongst other patrons at this time were Colonel Harvey of Castle Semple who commissioned a view of his Castle and lake (SA 1838, untraced), Sir George MacPherson Grant of Ballindalloch Castle who acquired a small oil from the 1837 SA show (Cat No 14) and APFAS which purchased no less than five of McCulloch's nine pictures from the 1838 SA exhibition. One of these, *Loch-an-Eilin*, was also chosen to be engraved for presentation to all APFAS subscribers the following year. Fraser explains that the title of this work is misleading because it was principally an imaginary composition, based on studies of trees made at Barncluith (near Hamilton) and into which the distant loch and castle were introduced at a later stage on the advice of an artist-friend. Throughout his career McCulloch produced landscapes only loosely based on actual locations.

McCulloch was not entirely happy with life in the limited society of Hamilton. Writing in November 1837[37] to his Edinburgh friend the landscape painter J F Williams, he sounds positively lonely and desperate for news from the capital '. . . I feel at present like a Traveller resting in his onward journey and looking around him for the joyous Company of Friends that had started with him in the morning how many of the best and dearest have dropt off and pursued paths of their own. Death has stopt others . . .'. He was probably referring here to the recent death of Robert Macnish during the influenza epidemic that January and whose loss must have contributed to McCulloch's feeling of isolation. Macnish had been educated in Hamilton before studying medicine at Glasgow University, and according to his biographer D M Moir[38], was fond of the natural scenery around Hamilton. He would have supported McCulloch's plan to move there and happily travelled the ten miles or so from Glasgow to visit his friend. As well as enjoying cultural outings and walks in the Forest the two men had acquired a reputation as pranksters. A moonlight ride on a 'borrowed' elephant and a masquerade as the sons of O'Connell (the Chartist leader) are recalled by most of McCulloch's biographers. Of the first escapade Fraser writes: 'Another exploit of this same period was a moonlight ride of the two friends on the elephant of a travelling caravan through the streets of Hamilton, disturbing the sleeping inhabitants by all sorts of mad cantrips as they passed along abreast of the first-floor windows'.

The loss of this congenial companion doubtless influenced the tone of McCulloch's next remarks in the letter to J F Williams: 'I heard you had been very ill and it gave me very great pleasure to hear from W Jardine[39] that you are now completely recovered, and that I am likely to have the pleasure of your company for many a mile yet on the journey of life . . .'. He continues with a barrage of questions about the forthcoming Scottish Academy exhibition and asks for news of D O Hill, Thomas Duncan (1807-45) and the rest of the Edinburgh artists.

His melancholy mood was soon to be shaken off by his election as full Academician on 10 February 1838[40]. In addition laudatory reviews of his 1838 exhibits appeared in the *Scotsman* on 21 February, and the influential Professor Wilson applauded him in a public speech[41]. After years of struggle McCulloch was at last beginning to achieve widespread recognition. He was selling many of his exhibited works and also attracting commissions from prominent people. In April that year a public dinner was held in Hamilton Town Hall in his honour '. . . Horatio McCulloch Esq, on the occasion of his departure for Edinburgh, to express admiration of his conduct as a gentleman, and his ability as an artist'[42].

EDINBURGH 1838-47

McCulloch's first home in Edinburgh was a modest terraced house in the New Town, at 12 Howard Place. As before his household comprised himself, his mother and his sister Elizabeth[43]. On 9 Sept 1838, not long after he had settled in, 'Hory' was writing excitedly to 'Dan' [Macnee][44] about a sketching trip to Castle Campbell (see Cat No 18) and congratulating Macnee on his success in that year's Dilettanti Society exhibition. He continues '. . . the greatest man in the world is in Edin just now I mean Sir David [? Wilkie] I would very much like to see him and I expect I will.' Whether he did meet Wilkie is not known, but McCulloch was certainly well established in the cultural life of the capital. Before the 1838 move he had made many contacts in Edinburgh and with his election as Academician his status in the artistic community was assured. The letter concludes 'Harvie [*sic*] and Duncan are both getting on with their pictures but John will have told you about them. My picture of Cadzow Castle has [? again] been sold in the Newcastle Exhibition[45], they tell me it is a great favourite there . . .'.

McCulloch flourished in the lively atmosphere of Edinburgh and was obviously delighted to be amongst so many other artists after his exile in Hamilton. In the letter quoted above he mentions that 'John' was with him on the trip to Castle Campbell. This was probably John Crawford Brown (1805-67) the Glasgow-born landscape painter. Brown had been a near neighbour of McCulloch in Laurieston around 1830, was a committee member of the Dilettanti Society between 1834 and 1838 and followed McCulloch to Edinburgh in 1841-2 moving into 22 Howard Place, just up the road from Horatio.

In November 1842[46] McCulloch recommends Brown to the publisher Thomas Constable as 'an artist of great talent and a neighbour of mine'. The two men were evidently fond of each other's company for Fraser tells us that Brown spent the autumn of 1844 at Invercoe with McCulloch and another close friend, William Borthwick Johnstone (1804-68), and it is likely that Brown accompanied McCulloch on other sketching trips. Johnstone, lawyer turned artist, who later became Curator of the National Gallery of Scotland, shared many enthusiasms with McCulloch besides painting. Both men were keen collectors of antiques, antiquities and works of art, and both had wide literary and historical interests[47]. But whilst Johnstone was author of several learned articles and of the first National Gallery of Scotland catalogue, the sole expression of McCulloch's creative powers was painting.

In 1839 he made what was possibly his first trip south of the border but unfortunately there is very little

McCulloch and W B Johnstone (Cat No 64)

documentation of this excursion. Fraser outlines McCulloch's itinerary by listing visits to the Lake District, Derbyshire, part of South Wales and London but the only English title amongst his eight exhibits at the RSA the following spring was *Goodriche Court and Castle, on the River Wye* (untraced). This was dismissed by the *Scotsman* critic in words which one suspects did not greatly offend the artist 'Mr McCulloch has treated the subject too much after the manner of a Highland Loch . . . we cannot conceal that we prefer seeing Mr McCulloch amid the forests and on the moors of his own country'[48]. McCulloch's exhibits for the rest of his life were all pictures of Scotland.

In 1841 annual exhibitions of modern art resumed in Glasgow, organised by the recently formed West of Scotland Academy. McCulloch evidently decided to forget his earlier quarrel with the Glasgow art establishment for he was represented by two landscapes in the first

exhibition. He was rewarded by the following comment in the *Glasgow Courier*: 'No 69 [of Cadzow Forest] is a large, noble landscape, by Mr Horatio M'Culloch. In former times we have spoken of this gentleman in terms of both praise and censure. We can safely add that we have now nothing to say of him which it does not "become a friend to say and a kinsman to hear". His career as an artist has been highly honourable to him. From boyhood his aim was to be a great painter. His enthusiasm was of the highest, but it was well seated: it was abiding — enduring; and it has endured and borne him through many difficulties. However much and often he may have taken the pet with his critics — and with us among the number — he never took the pet with his art; . . . The painting which has led us to speak thus of an old friend, is worthy of Mr M'Culloch's high reputation. The greater part of it is wood and foliage — all managed with great care, producing an unerring effect. We hope that some one of our wealthy friends, will secure this admirable painting. . . . Fifty years hence and it will command four times its present price'. This prediction was far from the truth. McCulloch's prices reached a peak in the 1860s and 70s then progressively dropped as a new generation of artists with a radically different approach to landscape came to the fore.

The picture was in fact purchased by The Glasgow and West of Scotland Association for the Promotion of the Fine Arts[49], a body newly set up along similar lines to the Edinburgh Association (APFAS), and which was succeeded in 1848 by The Art Union of Glasgow.

It seems that McCulloch as well as 'taking the pet' had also taken notice of his earlier critics, or at least had happened to choose the approach they recommended, for he was now producing more 'finished' work for the exhibitions. In the 1840s he was still making broadly painted on-the-spot oil studies (eg Cat Nos 28, 29) but had learnt not to send these to the annual exhibitions but to use them as the basis for more carefully worked compositions for public display. Later, the preliminary studies themselves (eg Cat No 48) became more painstaking, and some of these were exhibited.

The next 'fault' to be fastened upon by the art journalists was his ineptness as a figure painter. His 1842 RSA exhibit *A Road scene on the Banks of Loch Long*[50] prompted the following notice in the *Scotsman*: 'The left part of this landscape, including the road with cattle, the trees in the middle distance & hills beyond, is in Macculloch's happiest manner. It is full of air and sweetly natural; but the rest of the picture appears to us less masterly. The figure of the cow-herd we may also hint is not good; but great excellence in landscape and in figures . . . is a rare gift'. Judging from the clumsily drawn figures in

Bothwell Castle (Cat No 15) this criticism was deserved.

McCulloch may have taken this to heart, for he seldom introduced prominent figure groups into his pictures, and when he did he sometimes invited a colleague to paint them. For example in the Edinburgh exhibition held soon after McCulloch's death in 1867, No 22 was *'Study from Nature at Dollar* — the figures by James Drummond RSA', No 33, *'Edinburgh Castle from the Water of Leith,* 1855 . . . The figures painted by Gourlay Steel' and 51 *'Study from Nature at Balerno Burn,* 1849, painted on the spot — Figures by Erskine Nicol, ARA'. Since the catalogue was written by McCulloch's old friend William Davidson Clark (?-1873), these statements are likely to have derived from first-hand knowledge. The collaborations in these instances date to McCulloch's most successful years and may reflect as much his wish to encourage younger or less fortunate artists as his inability to complete the painting for himself[51]. In such works as *Perth from the South* (Cat No 23), *The Clyde at Erskine Ferry* (Cat No 22), *The Cuillins from Ord* (Cat No 40) the figure groups are quite adequate as reminders that man is usually present in a landscape at least in the more accessible parts of Scotland. McCulloch's paintings of the wilder and more remote regions — Loch Katrine, Glencoe — are deliberately devoid of human life.· Here the only inhabitants shown are animals.

In the mid 1840s he was presumably completing all his pictures without assistance and was living on a fairly modest scale, although Fraser hints rather disapprovingly at McCulloch's tendency to extravagance in both financial and personal habits. There are many references to his popularity as a generous and loyal friend, a genial host and lively conversationalist. From the few untidily scrawled letters which survive McCulloch emerges as impulsive, disorganised (his pictures were usually submitted for exhibition at the very last minute) and constantly hard up, even later in life when he was earning quite large sums of money.

In April 1842 we find McCulloch's name heading the list of Edinburgh artists' signatures in a letter to the Editor of *The Art Union* in London. The letter was in response to accusations of favouritism directed at APFAS because of its nationalistic purchasing policy and to suggestions that the Scottish artists were actively involved in this discrimination. McCulloch and friends were anxious to declare their innocence and their wish for 'fair and open competition'.

Nevertheless APFAS determined to pursue its original aim of promoting Scottish art[52] which was fortunate for McCulloch who benefited considerably from the steady patronage of both the Edinburgh and Glasgow Associa-

Detail from BOTHWELL CASTLE 1837 (Cat No 15)

ROSLIN CASTLE engraving after McCulloch 1843

ations. To supplement this source of income he continued to produce work for illustrated books. In Dec 1842 lack of funds prompted him to press Thomas Constable for payment of £12 12 for a small oil of *Roslyn Castle* which the publisher had commissioned[53].

This financial crisis was soon relieved by two purchases on the part of APFAS from the 1843 RSA exhibition which gave McCulloch £230 in all. This allowed him to indulge in the trip to London that summer to see his work hung at the Royal Academy for the first and only time. This new venture was largely due to the recent election as RA of his old acquaintance David Roberts, who was now a successful figure in the London art world.

It was more than twenty years now since the young McCulloch and Daniel Macnee first admired Roberts' work at Glasgow's Theatre Royal and they would have been aware of his achievements in London and heard news of his exploits as an intrepid traveller during the

VIEW OF THE COAST OF SLEAT, ISLE OF SKYE lithograph after McCulloch 1850

intervening years. Moreover, Roberts had kept in close touch with Edinburgh friends, had sent work for exhibition at the RSA and visited the city quite frequently. His election as RA in 1841 led to a place on the hanging committee of that institution — good news indeed for his artist-colleagues in Edinburgh. It prompted Macnee to write to Roberts in April 1843[54] as follows: ' . . . Our friend M'Culloch has sent two pictures [to the Royal Academy] . . . I wished him to write to you saying he had sent them but in case he has not done so I have taken the liberty. I know he was afraid to write to you about his pictures in case you might think him a bore but I am sure if it is in your power you will see at least that his pictures are not altogether overlooked for I should think in the multitude of pictures such a thing not unlikely'. As it turned out McCulloch's pictures were accepted, but according to Fraser 'they were badly placed, and he never sent again'.

This is another hint at an aspect of McCulloch's character which had already emerged in the Glasgow dispute of 1835; that he was quick to take offence and likely to react impetuously without considering the future consequences of his actions. Although he later occasionally sent work to other London venues his avoidance of the Royal Academy is one of the prime reasons for his obscurity outside Scotland, both during his lifetime and ever since.

Despite this McCulloch was interested in and influenced by the work of his English contemporaries. Now, in 1844, he is reproved for 'misplaced admiration for Calcott [*sic*] and some other English landscape painters of high name'. This is the *Scotsman* critic again (16 March), who seems to be suggesting that visits to England are to be avoided for fear of contamination through confrontation with English scenery and worse still with English art.

It is difficult to judge the truth behind this criticism because none of the artist's 1844 RSA pictures has been traced[55], and other reviewers were full of praise for that year's exhibits[56]. McCulloch himself admitted his admiration for Callcott (Fraser p 26) and he is recorded too[57] as holding John Linnell and Clarkson Stanfield, and, inevitably, Claude and Turner, in high regard. Fraser however (p 36) comments that McCulloch was too much influenced by popular opinion, even in his choice of artists 'it was the works of men who had gained reputation whose merits he especially recognised and appreciated. Turner, Callcott and Copley Fielding were his favourites — not the men who were fighting an up-hill fight, such as Constable, Cox, Muller or Linnell'. McCulloch's own collection of more than 350 paintings, prints and drawings[58], although dictated to some extent by financial considerations and availability, gives some idea of his preferences. It consisted mostly of works by British artists with a few pieces attributed to 17th century Dutch masters. Earlier British painters include Richard Wilson, Sir Joshua Reynolds, Thomas Girtin and John Constable[59] as well as the older generation of Scottish artists, Sir William Allan, Alexander Nasmyth, Rev Thomson and H W Williams. Callcott, Francia, Prout, J D Harding and other English artists are outnumbered by McCulloch's Scottish friends and contemporaries.

Whatever influences came from England, McCulloch's vision of the Highlands as expressed in his exhibition pictures of the mid to late 1840s was highly individual. It prompted George Monro to write in 1846 'There is exquisite truth and tenderness in the landscapes of M'Culloch who seems to have caught the very soul of Highland scenery'[60]. *Misty Corries — Haunts of the Red Deer* (Cat No 30) illustrates well the artist's response to the dramatic effects of stormy weather in the Scottish mountains. He was fortunate that his fondness for painting the wilder parts of his country coincided with public taste. His principal private patrons at this time were Glasgow businessmen[61] and increasingly his exhibited works had been commissioned and paid for before the general public saw them.

In contrast to the grand Highland views, in the 1840s McCulloch also tried his hand at townscapes, perhaps with the idea of publishing a series of engraved views. As it turned out only one such engraving seems to have been produced (Cat No 32). More momentous both for his personal future and for his professional reputation, was his inclusion as one of the artists reproduced in *Scotland Delineated* (1847-54) an ambitious lithographic project undertaken by the London publisher Joseph Hogarth. One of McCulloch's contributions was *View of the Coast of Sleat, Isle of Skye*, the result of a first visit to the island where he found a new supply of spectacular subjects and where he met his future wife, Marcella McLellan[62].

MARRIAGE AND SUCCESS 1848-1857

After his marriage McCulloch moved his household along the street to his friend J C Brown's house at 22 Howard Place, whilst Brown took up residence at 6 Quality Street, Leith. McCulloch soon moved house again, in 1849, to 54 Inverleith Row. It is impossible not to wonder whether his sister Elizabeth now aged 38 (and perhaps his mother too if she was still alive) found it difficult to adapt to the new régime and therefore a larger home was essential for the happiness of all concerned. When the 1851 census return[63] was compiled for the night of 30 March the inhabitants of 54 Inverleith Row were Horatio McCulloch, head of the family, landscape painter, aged 44, Marcella McCulloch wife, aged 27, Elizabeth McCulloch, sister, aged 40, Isabella Mclennan mother-in-law (widow) aged 70[64], Elizabeth McGill aged 23 kitchen maid and Sarah Wilson aged 20 housemaid.

Very little is known about Marcella other than her age and place of birth (Sleat, Isle of Skye) and that she and McCulloch had no children. Soon after his death in 1867 she emigrated to Australia[65]. Fraser describes her briefly as 'a woman rich in the best qualities of the heart'.

Marcella evidently resolved to bring order into her new husband's haphazard management of his finances for there survives an account book[66] documenting all picture sales and other receipts from January 1848 until November 1865, when it comes to an abrupt end. Most of the entries are in a neat, slightly tremulous handwriting, presumably Marcella's. The account book is today a valuable source of information about patrons, prices, pupils and apprentices, and the part played by picture dealers as financial providers.

The first two of McCulloch's occasional pupils are recorded in 1850; in May he received £6.6s from a Miss Forbes for six lessons and in December, the same amount from Mr Ware[67]. More importantly, for the whole of 1850 and 1851 he had an apprentice, Edward Hargitt (1835-95) who later made his name as a landscape painter in London, and in May 1853 he was paid £30 'from Mr Martin[68] of Glasgow for his son's apprenticeship'.

What part the apprentices played in McCulloch's studio routine is not known, but the fact that no others were taken on perhaps suggests that McCulloch preferred to advise and encourage younger artists rather than undertake their formal training. Later on, however, there were more pupils: Mr Hay[69] in 1856, who had eleven lessons at a pound a time, and in Dec 1860 Mr William Henderson[70] and Mr Smart[71] each paid £52.10s, the latter for 'three months painting lessons'. James Alfred Aitken (1846-97) the Glasgow landscape painter was also reputedly

Thomas Annan HORATIO McCULLOCH *c*1860

a pupil; some of the unspecified payments from 'Mr Aitken' in the 1860s may refer to this circumstance.

Partnerships with other artists have already been mentioned (p 00) — James Drummond (1816-77), Gourlay Steell (1819-94) and Erskine Nicol (1825-1904). That McCulloch collaborated with Drummond[72] is not surprising for the two artists shared a passion for Scottish history, and both were avid collectors of antiquities, books and art objects, as were several of their contemporaries notably D O Hill and Joseph Noel Paton (1821-1901). His connection with Gourlay Steell has yet to be investigated, but there is documentary evidence of the fatherly interest that McCulloch took in the career of Erskine Nicol. Letters written in 1861 from Nicol to Sir James Lumsden[73] suggest that their 'mutual friend Mr Macculloch' had encouraged Lumsden to patronise Nicol. (McCulloch himself owned three works by Nicol[74].)

McCulloch's biographer, the landscape painter Alexander Fraser (1828-99) was a close enough friend for his account of McCulloch's way of life in the 1850s and 60s to be taken as first hand. Fraser writes 'He was now on

intimate terms with most of his fellow-townsmen eminent in science or literature. He kept almost open house: at almost any hour his friends and his friends friends, were received with a most kindly welcome. Nor did the presence of several visitors at a time in his painting-room seem to interfere with his work'. Fraser is referring to McCulloch's years at 6 Danube Street a graceful residence in the west of the New Town where he lived between 1854 and 1862. Here despite the social whirl there was an established daily routine: '. . . from ten till between three and four, was spent in his painting room. After his day's work he went out for an hour's walk, in the course of which he would look in at any sale of works of art, or articles of taste he might take an interest in, or at a friend's painting room; this latter however not often. Between five and six he dined. If he had no visitors, the evening would be spent reading, or in making sepia sketches of ideas he might purpose working up into pictures; and if any artist friend came in and joined him at his work, McCulloch would work all the better for what to most men would have been an interruption. But, more usually about eight, visitors would drop in, either accidentally or by special invitation; and round his supper-table were frequently to be met his townsmen most eminent in literature, science and art. An evening spent by a stranger at McCulloch's house was not likely to be forgotten. His welcome so hearty, his manner so frank and friendly, and his conversation, rich in references to literature, full of anecdote and of illustrations gathered from nature and from long intercourse with gifted friends, were always delightful'.

The many examples of McCulloch's work which survive from the 1850s and 60s show a change in style which can be attributed partly to the demands of public taste but which also represents his own development as an artist within the context of new ideas and attitudes to landscape painting. (For example he owned a copy of Ruskin's *Elements of drawing* and probably attended that influential critic's Edinburgh lectures in 1853.)

The change is most obvious in the artist's on-the-spot studies. *On the Water of Leith* (Cat No 35) and *Castle Campbell* (Cat No 36) both done in 1853 are carefully composed and minutely observed pieces of painting, the evidence of many hours spent before the subject; most of the earlier out of door work so far located gives the impression at least, of having been dashed off in an hour or so.

Fraser, who only knew McCulloch in the latter part of his life, asserts that 'While his work on his pictures [ie his studio productions] was swift and dashing, his work out of doors on his more important studies was slow and thoughtful . . .'.

Sam Bough CADZOW FOREST 1855

The preparatory study for *Loch Lomond* (Cat No 48) when compared with the finished oil (Cat No 47) illustrates how it was possible for McCulloch to be 'swift and dashing' in the studio. In the process of painting the study he has so thoroughly explored the subject that, despite changes to the foreground, the large version is essentially a repetition of the smaller work.

McCulloch was still in the habit of spending several months each year sketching in the Highlands. In the summer of 1854 for example he was in Oban with a new patron David Hutcheson (see Cat No 39) and by 30 September had crossed over to the Isle of Skye, a regular resort for the artist since his marriage. A result of this particular visit was the careful watercolour study of Knock Castle (Cat No 38) which was used as the basis for his 1855 RSA exhibit of that subject. The critics were at this period unanimous in praising just about everything McCulloch produced. Of the Knock Castle oil *The Art Journal* critic wrote '. . . There is nothing in the exhibition equal to the feeling and truth in the foreground. . . . The whole picture is suffused with the clear cold breezy air of a northern shore'. The same writer however draws attention to the merits of the younger generation of Scot-

tish landscape-painters, in particular Alexander Fraser and J C Wintour (1825-82). He also notices McCulloch's former apprentice, Edward Hargitt, John Milne Donald (1819-66) and Sam Bough (1822-78).

Mention of the last named is significant for only three years later we find *The Art Journal* reviewer suggesting that Sam Bough is overtaking McCulloch 'In landscape Horatio M'Culloch, E Crawford, T Faed, Houston and Perigal all sustain their well-merited reputation; but amongst the younger artists several are treading closely upon their steps. Among these by far the most successful is Mr Samuel Bough . . . His versatility is amazing . . . We risk but little in predicting a brilliant future for this industrious and versatile young artist'[75].

The *Scotsman* critic too is a little cool about McCulloch that year[76] and regrets that the artist is unable to complete his 'great picture of the Clyde' in time for the exhibition (see Cat No 44).

These remarks came after a well-publicised squabble between McCulloch and Sam Bough which soured their friendship and allegedly split the Edinburgh art world into two camps[77]; the art establishment, including D O Hill and Sir George Harvey, supported McCulloch.

FINAL YEARS 1858-67

In June 1858 we find McCulloch and Macnee in London visiting artist-friends and undoubtedly also the Royal Academy exhibition. On 20 June David Roberts wrote to D R Hay 'I had a visit of Maculloch, who was here last week with MacNee . . .'[78] and a letter written about the same time to Roberts from John Phillip[79] reads '2 June 1 South Villas, Campden Hill, My dear Roberts, I hope you will come and meet MacNee McCulloch McCleese [*sic*] and a few others at the Garrick [Club] on Monday next at ½ after 6. Your presence will add much to their pleasure and to mine . . .'[80]. John Phillip (1817-67), the Aberdeenshire artist best known for his paintings of Spanish life, is named by Gilpin (*op cit*) as being on McCulloch's side in the quarrel with Sam Bough. A further indication that McCulloch and Phillip were good friends is that McCulloch received a painting and a pottery vase as gifts from Phillip.[81] There is evidence that McCulloch was in London again in June 1861[82], and more visits not yet documented seem probable.

Back in Scotland, in November 1861 the Glasgow papers were full of the news of the opening of the Glasgow Institute of the Fine Arts' first exhibition of the works of modern masters. The *Glasgow Gazette* of 16 November applauded this event as long overdue and went on to praise McCulloch's 'magnificent landscapes'. Two days earlier the *Glasgow Herald* had filled an entire column with an enthusiastic tribute to McCulloch's genius concluding 'The Institute is fortunate in having received five pictures by him of so much character. They are enough to show the visitor that Mr McCulloch has borne away with him somewhat of nature's opulence, and embodied upon canvas somewhat of the softness and imperishable beauty of the world'.

Fortified by the adulation of his compatriots McCulloch was probably undismayed by the *Art Union*'s dismissive comment the next spring '. . . Macculloch, as usual in his later pictures of highland scenery, substitutes prettiness for grandeur'. The Scottish art journalists continued to eulogise up to and after his death.

Towards the end of 1862 McCulloch moved house once again, for the last time. His new home was St Colm Villa, Trinity, to the north of Edinburgh. Fraser attributes the move to lack of space at Danube Street and to a wish for more seclusion. Additional space was required to house McCulloch's large collection and ill-health was probably another reason. His treasures included Scottish and Egyptian antiquities, English and continental porcelain and Wedgwood pottery, glass, ivories, enamels, silver, jewellery, coins and medals and Tassie medallions. The wide-ranging character of this collection was matched by the contents of his library. There were many volumes of Scottish and English literature and history, books on theatre, music, foreign travel and, not surprisingly, a number of gazetteers and Scottish topographical works. Although it is impossible to know when a particular volume was added to the library some significance must be read into his owning copies of Claude's *Liber Veritatis,* Constable's *English Landscape Scenery* and Turner's *South Coast* as well as the edition of Scott's poems illustrated by Turner. That he had a copy of Robert Hills' *Etchings of Cattle, deer, sheep etc* calls for investigation — animals derived from Hills may occur in McCulloch's works.

He also owned several scrapbooks of engravings, and others containing 'Calotypes, chiefly landscapes' and 'numerous portraits of eminent Scottish Artists, scenes from Life, and views from Nature' and 'a selection from D O Hill's photographs'. McCulloch has left no clue as to his attitude to photography, but he was certainly fully aware of developments in Edinburgh from the early days of Hill and Adamson through to the 1860s; one of his oldest friends William Donaldson Clark was a keen and talented amateur photographer[83]. Although McCulloch's 1865 painting of Loch Katrine (Cat No 52) was described as 'photographic' in *The Art Journal*, he must have felt secure in the knowledge that photography could not reproduce nature as he did, in full colour and on a grand scale.

During the 1860s, although he produced a succession of large and impressive exhibition pictures McCulloch's health was in decline. In 1860 the local press noted 'a severe attack of illness' which was the return of a paralysis which according to Fraser had first affected him in 1850. Early in 1866 he had a more severe attack, and another the next winter was followed by a fatal third seizure from which he died on 24 June 1867 at St Colm 'in the presence of his sorrowing wife and several friends'[84]. His doctor, Robert Bowes Malcolm, attributed McCulloch's death to 'softening of the brain' and 'paralysis for several years'[85]. Despite what seems to have been a lingering illness, the artist continued to paint whenever he was well enough. One obituarist even claims that his 'vigorous and busy pencil . . . only dropped from his hand in the hour of his death'[86]. He was buried at Warriston cemetery near his first Edinburgh home and close to the Water of Leith where he had spent many hours sketching (see Cat No 35). The grave is marked by a Celtic cross designed by James Drummond (see p 23) and erected in 1873 by subscription. At the base of the monument on one side is a bas-relief of a palette and brushes and laurel wreath, on the other a portrait of a dog. McCulloch's dogs are almost better documented than is his family:

McCulloch's grave in Warriston Cemetery

whilst he owned no portraits of his wife, parents or sister, he had a painting by Macnee of 'Oscar' a Skye terrier, several dog pictures by John Sheriff and 'A Skye Terrier' by Thomas Duncan[87]; in 1856 John Glass exhibited at the RSA (465) *Bessy, a terrier, the property of Horatio McCulloch Esq RSA*[88]. We learn from Gilpin's account of the quarrel with Sam Bough, that McCulloch's Skye terrier was allowed to follow his master into the Academy on touching-up days (and that Bough encouraged his bull-dog to menace the smaller animal). The fate of the pet dog after McCulloch's death is not known, but his property was soon sold, his debts paid off and his widow departed forthwith for Australia. The proceeds of the sale of the artist's personal estate had amounted to £3,584 11s[89].

NOTES TO INTRODUCTION

1 Contemporary spellings of the surname, even by the artist himself, are inconsistent. Variations include M'Culloch, Macculloch and MacCulloch. McCulloch is used in this catalogue except when quoting from a text in which another form occurs.

2 His name is not included in the index to births registered with the Established Church of Scotland (NRH) (it might therefore be found amongst the registers of one of the nonconformist churches). Most biographers, including Fraser, give 1805 (Nov) as the date of birth as does his grave memorial in Warriston Cemetery (see p 25). The cemetery record of mortality records that he was 62, but his death certificate (NRH) states his age as 61 (June 1867). His birthplace is identified by William Young in *Glasgow Scraps* vol 11 p 39 (Mitchell Library, Glasgow). The earliest record of his father discovered so far is in *The Burgesses and Guild Brethren of Glasgow 1751-1846* ed James R Anderson, Edinburgh 1935 p 257 'M'Culloch, Alexander, Merchant, . . . as eldest son of Alexander McCulloch, weaver, Port Patrick, 14 May 1808'. The name does not appear in the *Post Office Glasgow Directory* until 1811 (apart from an Alexander McCulloch, grocer, listed between 1801 and 1804) and the first certain identification is the 1813 entry.

3 A move to nearby St Andrew's Street in 1817 coincided with a change in the structure of the company, which became McCulloch, Dewar & Co. Subsequent changes of address are recorded in the *Post Office Glasgow Directory,* as are the names of other McCullochs whose relationship to Horatio's family, if any, has not been determined.

4 According to Chambers vol 3 p 11: 'His first regular instructor in his future profession was Mr Alexander Watt, teacher of drawing in Glasgow'. The *Post Office Glasgow Directory* lists 'Watt Alexander, Glasgow Academy, 48 Dunlop Street', between 1818 and 1822 after which there are several changes of address until 1829, 13 West George St, the last entry for Watt in the Directory. Notices in the *Glasgow Courier* for 28 March and 3 Oct 1818 inform us that Watt took over the practice of 'the late Mr Denholm' and that his classes covered 'drawing, painting, perspective, architecture etc'. On 21 July 1818 his advertisement included 'A boy who has a taste for drawing wanted as an apprentice'.

5 First advertised in the *Glasgow Courier* 2 Jan 1810 and frequently readvertised up to Sept that year. It was exhibited 'At the large wooden building, south side of the New Theatre, Queen Street'.

6 He first advertised as a teacher on 9 May 1812 in the *Glasgow Courier*: 'Mr Knox having now resolved to dedicate some portion of his time to teaching the art of painting, will commence on the 1st June, in that [sic] house No 9 Buchanan Street'. By 1817 his drawing school was at 40 Dunlop St.

7 See Pieter van der Merwe 'Roberts and the Theatre' in Guiterman and Llewellyn *David Roberts* London 1986 pp 33-6.

8 His 'new and appropriately spendid scenery' for Sheridan Knowles' play *Virginius* is described in the *Glasgow Courier* 1 Feb 1820.

9 Geoffrey Crayon Jun (alias John Strang) *A Glance at the exhibitions of the Works of Living Artists . . .* Glasgow 1830.

10 Alexander Smith 'The Minister Painter' in P Alexander *Last Leaves* Edinburgh 1868 (Thanks are due to Simon Berry for this reference) see also W Baird *John Thomson of Duddingston* Edinburgh 1895 and R W Napier *John Thomson of Duddingston* Edinburgh 1919.

11 For an account of this society and of the early Glasgow exhibitions see Brydall ch XVII; see also Hamish Miles 'Early Exhibitions in Glasgow' *Scottish Art Review* VIII 3, 4 1962.

12 Man of letters and with a private income, John Strang (1795-1863), published widely on literature, the arts and local subjects and was City Chamberlain of Glasgow from 1834 until his death.

13 No reviews have been found for the first exhibition, and for the second, reviews (in *Glasgow Courier* Aug-Nov 1829) concentrate on the English artists John Glover (1767-1849) and J V Barber (1787-1838).

14 Opp p 66 *Cora Lynn, Glasgow from the East* and *Bothwell Castle* (the last probably his 1831 DS exhibit) and opp p 114 *The Clyde from Dalnottar, Loch Lomond* and *Inveraray* (1831 RSA and 1830 Glasgow exhibits). Views of Staffa and Ireland might also have been McCulloch's. The artists' names are not identified against individual engraved images.

15 The names of purchasers from the Dilettanti Society Exhibitions were usually listed in the *Glasgow Courier* after the close of the exhibition. Amongst McCulloch's early patrons were D C Rait, a Glasgow goldsmith and jeweller who was on the committee of the Dilettanti Society, Rev Hugh Heugh DD a prominent Glasgow churchman, Lorraine Wilson of Wilson Shaw & Co another Dilettanti Society committee member and John Fleming of Claremont.

16 James Hedderwick *Backward Glances* Edinburgh and London 1891 p 164.

17 His work for Napier *c*1833 is mentioned in James Napier *Life of Robert Napier of West Shandon* Edinburgh and London MCMIV p 51.

18 James Hedderwick *op cit* and 'Old Kirkintilloch Lairds' in *Kirkintilloch Herald* 22 July 1914 (I am grateful to Jackie van Bavel for the latter reference). See also Cat Nos 2 and 7 for more about Thomson of Bellfield.

19 *Caledonian Mercury* quoted in *Glasgow Herald* 3 March 1834.

20 Proposed by D O Hill and seconded by George Harvey, in RSA Minute Book 1830-43 p 115 (RSA Library).

21 29 May 1835, in RSA Minute Book 1830-43 p 159 (RSA Library). The Mr Graham referred to was the portrait painter John Graham-Gilbert (1794-1866).

22 Of which no copies appear to have survived. It is likely that it was suppressed.

23 *A Criticism on the Pictures in the Glasgow Exhibition;* . . . Glasgow 1835.

24 It was purchased from the DS exh by Neale Thomson of Camphill (Fraser p 21) and exh 1867 Edinburgh Clark Exh (1) lent by Mrs Thomson of Camphill. Now untraced. The usual spelling of the place-name is Rouken Glen (a notable Glasgow Park).

25 The extracts which he quotes from *A Glance* reveal that it was partly written in the style used by Professor Wilson in the popular *Blackwoods* series *Noctes Ambrosianae* — *ie* in the form of a dialogue between himself (Christopher North), The Shepherd (The Ettrick Shepherd, James Hogg the poet) and other characters — but here the speakers are called Sec and Spec.

26 Although McCulloch's name is strangely absent from biographies of Wilson by his daughter Mrs Gordon (1862) and by Elsie Swann (1934).

27 In *Recreations of Christopher North* 1842 and subsequent editions.

28 eg SA 1833 (17); SA 1834 (123).

29 Named by a previous occupant, John Allan, grocer and spirit dealer, and marked on J Wood's *Plan of Hamilton* 1819.

30 Pigot & Co's *Directory* 1837 p 629.

31 D M Moir *The Modern Pythagorean . . . Robert Macnish* Edinburgh 1838 vol 1 p 376.

32 For an account of the 10th Duke's improvements to the Palace see A A Tait 'The Duke of Hamilton's Palace' *The Burlington Magazine* July 1983 pp 394-402.

33 Information provided by Jill Mackenzie 1987 who kindly supplied lists of the pictures likely to have been seen by visitors to the Palace c1835. The collection was sold by Christie's 17 June-20 July 1882, and the Palace demolished 1919-26.

34 John Hayes *The Landscape Paintings of Thomas Gainsborough . . .* vol 2 pp 360-1.

35 W G Constable *Richard Wilson* London and Cambridge Mass. 1953 p 220.

36 Hamilton Palace Visitors Book GAG (*23-44ad*).

37 Letter in NGS (I am grateful to Lindsay Errington for informing me of this source).

38 *Op cit* vol 1 pp 4-7.

39 Probably Sir William Jardine (1800-74) naturalist and brother-in-law of McCulloch's employer in Edinburgh, W H Lizars.

40 RSA Minute Book 1830-43 p 155 (RSA Library).

41 APFAS *Report* for 1837-8.

42 *Glasgow Courier* 26 April 1838.

43 1841 census return (NRH 685/2) McCulloch himself was not at home but his mother and sister are recorded as Margaret Watson aged 55 and Elizabeth McCulloch aged 25 (Elizabeth was actually about 30 years of age in June 1841. Even though ages were adjusted to the nearest 5, 30 would have been more accurate).

44 Letter written on same sheet as a letter to Macnee from Jas Jardine (RSA Library).

45 Along with other Scottish artists, McCulloch sent work to provincial exhibitions, as well as to London and Dublin (see list of EXHIBITED WORKS 1828-68 p 31).

46 Letter in NLS (3109 182)

47 See cat of W B Johnstone sale, Chapman's Edinburgh 6, 8 and 9 Feb 1869. The collection included numerous works by McCulloch, many of which are catalogued as 'study from nature'.

48 *Scotsman* 4 March 1840.

49 *Glasgow Courier* 25 Nov 1841, where it is titled *Scene in Cadzow Forest*. See entry for Cat No 12 where Cadzow subjects are discussed.

50 Untraced; Lot 365 in Sotheby's Gleneagles sale 27, 28 Aug 1979 was identified as this picture, but its subject does not agree with the description quoted here. Lot 365 was probably McCulloch's 1843 RSA exhibit *36 Loch Katrine from the Boat House* (see entry for Cat No 52).

51 There is also evidence of McCulloch providing the landscape background for a specialist animal painter (McCulloch sale 7 Dec 1867 lot 122 'Sidney Cooper *Sheep in a landscape* (the landscape by M'Culloch)').

52 In its *Report* for 1841-2 APFAS defends its policies and in particular its decision to pay McCulloch £130 for a picture 'the largest sum yet paid by the Association for a landscape with the single exception of £150 which

was given to the late Rev Mr Thomson for one of his great efforts'.

53 Letter NLS (3109 161). *Roslyn Castle* was engraved for T D Lauder's *Royal Progress in Scotland* (1843). In 1841 a *Kilchurn Castle* engraved by R C Bell after McCulloch had been used by Blackie to illustrate Lawson's *Gazetteer of Scotland*.

54 NLS (2255 f71). Evidence of Roberts' interest in McCulloch is contained in a letter to D R Hay 18 March 1841 'How is McCulloch this year? has he a picture for the Royal Academy' (NLS Acc 8729 — information from Ian Gow 1985).

55 No 227 *A Dream of the Highlands* which prompted the comparison with Callcott was purchased by APFAS for £100 and awarded as a prize to L F MacKinnon, Jamaica (APFAS *Report*).

56 *Art Union* March 1844; *Glasgow Courier* 16 Nov 1844.

57 Obit in *The Art Journal* 1 Aug 1867.

58 Sold by Chapman's Edinburgh 7 and 9 Dec 1867.

59 This attribution (and doubtless several others) was almost certainly incorrect (see Fraser p 36).

60 *Scottish Art and National Encouragement* Edinburgh & London 1846 p 134.

61 eg William Dennistoun, and John Houldsworth of Coltness Iron Works.

62 The surname is uncertain. It is given as McLennan in some sources. The explanation may be that Marcella's mother's maiden name was McLennan or simply that the similarity between the two surnames has caused confusion: in the 1851 census the mother, who was from South Uist, is named McLennan, in 1861 McLellan. McLellan is a sept of the Macdonald clan and therefore more likely as a Skye surname.

63 NRH (CEN/RET 685/2).

64 McCulloch's mother is not listed. She may have died or merely been away that night, and the mother-in-law may have been on a visit rather than a permanent resident.

65 Document attached to a seal given by Marcella to the captain (or first mate) of the Australia-bound ship (GAG Dept of Archaeology *A.832*).

66 RSA Library (Thanks are due to Mrs Meta Viles and to the RSA for allowing the author to copy this important document).

67 It has not been possible to identify either Miss Forbes or Mr Ware.

68 Possibly Samuel Martin who exhibited watercolour landscapes at the GIFA 1866-70 from a Paisley address.

69 Possibly George Hay (1831-1912). See Caw p 261.

70 Possibly William Henderson who exhibited watercolours with the GIFA 1879-81.

71 Presumably John Smart (1839-99). See Caw pp 297-8.

72 For more about Drummond see Elizabeth S Cumming *James Drummond RSA* Exh Cat Canongate Tolbooth Museum, Edinburgh 1977.

73 Lumsden Papers Bundle 30 (GUA). See also index to PREVIOUS COLLECTIONS AND DONORS p 107.

74 McCulloch sale 9 Dec 1867 lots 185, 186, 237.

75 *The Art Journal* 1858 p 100.

76 *Scotsman* 13, 15 and 23 Feb 1858.

77 Sidney Gilpin *Sam Bough RSA* London 1905 pp 121-3.

78 Letter in NLS (information from Helen Guiterman 1985).

79 Probably also written in 1858, and certainly after 1851 when Phillip is first recorded at this address.

80 BM (MS ADD 42577) (Information from George A MacKenzie 1986).

81 McCulloch sale 7 Dec 1867 lot 70 'John Phillip RA Kate Nickleby (a present from the artist)' possibly the picture now in Aberdeen Art Gallery, and on the first day, 28 Nov, lot 213 'old Blue Wedgwood vase, with white figures, a gift from the late John Phillip RA'. John Phillip's sale at Christie Manson & Woods, 31 May 1867, listed three works by McCulloch:
Lot 35 *A village on a stream* (drawing) Bought Agnew £2 Lot 80 *A Scotch Lake Scene* (oil) Bought Brown £5 5s and Lot 85 *A Mountainous Landscape* (oil) Bought Brown £8 18s 6d
(Information from George A MacKenzie 1986).

82 Letter to David Roberts accepting a dinner invitation, dated 27 June 1861, address 25 Craven street (EUL).

83 See Sara Stevenson and Julie Lawson *Masterpieces of Photography from the Riddell Collection* Edinburgh SNPG 1986 pp 118-20.

84 Obit *Glasgow Daily Herald* 26 June 1867.

85 Register of Deaths, District of North Leith (NRH).

86 Annotated RSA reports 1850-83 (RSA Library).

87 All included in the sale of McCulloch's pictures, 7 and 9 Dec 1867.

88 Thanks are due to Lindsay Errington for this reference.

89 SRO SC 70/1/138.

CHRONOLOGY

1805	**Nov** Born Glasgow — parents Alexander McCulloch, merchant, and Margaret Watson
*c*1810	Sister Elizabeth born
1819-20	David Roberts scene painter at Theatre Royal, Glasgow
*c*1823	Tuition from John Knox, landscape-painter, Glasgow
*c*1824	To Cumnock, Ayrshire, with Daniel Macnee for employment decorating snuff-boxes
*c*1825-7	Edinburgh with Macnee for employment (colouring prints) with W H Lizars, engraver; copies watercolours by H W Williams
*c*1827-8	Returns to Glasgow on death of his father
1828	First exhibited work in Glasgow DS exhibition
1829	First exhibited work in Edinburgh at SA; destruction by fire of Theatre Royal, Glasgow
1830	First published criticism of his work
*c*1830-1	Visit to Isle of Bute
1831	Illustrations in Lumsden's *Steam-boat Companion*
1832	Committee member of DS
*c*1833	Visit to Isle of Arran; employment by Napier as decorator of steamship interiors; patronage from James Lumsden
1834	Visits to Inveraray and environs of Hamilton; sends work to Manchester (first exhibit outside Scotland); **12 Nov** elected ASA
1835	Committee member of DS; pamphlet controversy; moves to Hamilton; Glasgow Cathedral lithograph in Allan and Ferguson's *Views of Glasgow and Neighbourhood*
1836	**23 June** visit to Hamilton Palace with Macnish and Macnee
1837	**9 June** and **15 July** visits to Hamilton Palace
1838	**10 Feb** elected full Academician (SA); **April** farewell dinner Hamilton; **5 May** visit to Hamilton Palace; moves to Edinburgh; SA council member; illustrations in W Beattie's *Scotland*; **Sept** visit to Castle Campbell
1839	Tour of England and Wales (John Knox moves to Lake District); *Loch-an-Eilin* engraved for APFAS
1840	RSA council member
1841	*Kilchurn Castle* engraved for J P Lawson's *Gazetteer of Scotland*
1842	Letter in *The Art Union*
1843	Visit to London to see his first and only exhibits at RA; *Roslyn Castle* engraved for T D Lauder's *Royal Progress in Scotland*

*c*1844	Visit from John Wilson (1818-75) and sister (as recorded in letter in NLS, 9392 no 228)
1844	RSA council member; Invercoe with J C Brown and W B Johnstone
1845	RSA council member
1846	RSA council member; autumn trip to Glencoe via Loch Lomond
1847	First visit to Skye
*c*1847	Marriage to Marcella McLellan
1847-54	Illustrations in J P Lawson's *Scotland Delineated*
1848	**Jan** first entry in Account Book
1849	*Moonlight* engraved (mezzotint) for RAPFAS; *Kelso* engraving published; summer at Spylaw Bank with W B Johnstone
1850	In autumn suffers mild stroke whilst at Kelso; apprentice — Edward Hargitt
1851	RSA council member; *A Forest Glade* engraved for RAPFAS
1852	RSA council member
1853	**Sept** visit to Castle Campbell
1854	Summer and early autumn at Oban and in Skye
1856	Visit to Inverlochy Castle (Fort William)
1857	Autumn in Glasgow sketching River Clyde
1858	**June** visit to London with Macnee; RSA council member
1859	Autumn at Gairloch, Ross-shire; RSA council member
1860	**Feb** 'severe illness'; Loch Lomond visit
1861	*My Heart's in the Highlands* engraved for RAPFAS; **June** visit to London; Autumn visit to Loch Katrine
1862	Early summer visit to Bothwell Castle and Cadzow Forest
1863	*A Highland Loch — Mist resting on Mountains* engraved for RAPFAS; summer at *The Manse*, Trossachs (Loch Achray subjects)
1864	RSA council member
1865	Curator of RSA Library with Robert Herdman
1866	*The Trosachs* [sic] engraved for RAPFAS; Curator of RSA Library
1867	**24 June** death at St Colm, Trinity, Edinburgh **28 June** funeral, buried Warriston Cemetery **Nov** W D Clark's McCulloch Exhibition **Late Nov/Dec** sale of collection and library

EXHIBITED WORKS   1828-68

All entries are taken from the original catalogues. Exhibitions held in Edinburgh and Glasgow are always listed. Other places are listed only for years in which McCulloch is known to have exhibited.

McCulloch's address is given as it appears in the index to the exhibition catalogue except that the town name is included whether or not it is given in the original catalogue.

Titles of exhibits are reproduced as they appear in the catalogues. Other punctuation has been standardised. (Some peculiarities of spelling are probably due to McCulloch's appalling handwriting.)

This list does not include exhibitions for which no catalogues survive, and for which no precise information regarding McCulloch's exhibits has been found eg exhibitions of Art Union prize pictures in both Scotland and London.

The following exhibition centres were checked but with negative result: Birmingham, Bristol, Norwich.

Abbreviation	Exhibition
BELFAST NIAU	Northern Irish Art Union Information from Eileen Black 1987 (no surviving catalogues)
CARLISLE	The Carlisle Exhibition of Paintings & Sculpture Information from Laura Hamilton 1986
DUBLIN RHA	Royal Hibernian Academy Information from Ann M Stewart prior to publication of her index of RHA exhibitors, 1986
EDINBURGH SA	Scottish Academy
EDINBURGH RSA	Royal Scottish Academy Original catalogues checked by Janice Slater 1987
GLASGOW DS	Dilettanti Society Indexed by Jackie van Bavel 1983
GLASGOW WSA	West of Scotland Academy Indexed by Nancy Colvin 1984
GLASGOW GIFA	Glasgow Institute of the Fine Arts Indexed by GAG Fine Art Dept 1983
LIVERPOOL LA	Liverpool Academy Information from Mary Bennett 1985
LONDON BI	British Institution
LONDON FE	Free Exhibition of Modern Art
LONDON IE	International Exhibition
LONDON NI	The National Institution
LONDON RA	Royal Academy
MANCHESTER RMI	Royal Manchester Institution Information from Jane Farrington 1985
MANCHESTER AT	Art Treasures Exhibition
NEWCASTLE NES	North of England Society for the Promotion of the Fine Arts Information from Jane Vickers 1985 (catalogues consulted not a complete set)
PARIS UE	Universal Exhibition

1828

EDINBURGH SA

No exhibits

GLASGOW DS
Glasgow

85	Niddry Castle
139	View on the Stocky Muir
164	Study from Nature
184	Study from Nature near Cathcart

1829

EDINBURGH SA
No address given

128	View on the Clyde

GLASGOW DS
Glasgow

210	Coast scene – a sketch

1830

EDINBURGH SA

No exhibits

GLASGOW DS
Glasgow

11	Sketch near Cathcart
138	View on Loch Lomond
155	Groupe of Ash Trees near Luss
164	High Church, Glasgow, from Duke-Street

1831

EDINBURGH SA
Glasgow

9	A waterfall in Campsie Glen
160	Govine on the Clyde – Sunset
329	Inverary Castle
339	Boats on the Clyde – Sunset after a storm

GLASGOW DS
Glasgow

10	View on the Clyde
75	Bothwell Castle
176	Loch Fad, Isle of Bute
223	Portincross Castle
231	Kilmun, Holy Loch
304	View of Arran from Bute
316	Sketch, – near Rothsay
330	Loch Fad, Isle of Bute

1832

EDINBURGH SA

No exhibits

GLASGOW DS
Glasgow

3	Clyde, from Dunnotter Hill
27	Moor Scene – Rain passing off
45	Lochlomond
55	Head of Lochfine – Stormy effect
86	A Sunset
122	View of the Duke of Argyll's Fishing Cottage
142	Moor Scene
163	Scene in Argyllshire, with part of Lochawe and Ben Cruachan in the distance
223	View on the Kelvin
262	Cottage near Cambuslang

1833

EDINBURGH SA
Glasgow

17	Mearns Moor, from a Sketch painted on the spot
42	Lochlomond, near Balloch Ferry The property of C Baird Esq
150	Head of Loch Fine, Stormy effect The property of the Rev Dr Heugh
161	Ben Cruachan, Argyllshire

GLASGOW DS
Glasgow

30	Glen Scene – a Sketch The property of Lorraine Wilson Esq
45	Robert the Bruce's Glen, Arran
61	Coast Scene, a Sketch The property of Lorraine Wilson Esq
97	Landscape Composition
121	Glen Rosa – Arran 'The land where the clouds love to rest, Like the sheet of the dead on the mountain's cold breast' Mrs Robinson
136	Arran from Bute – Effect of the Sun breaking through a Rain-Cloud
157	Glen Shant – Sunset – Ben Noosh in the distance
273	Roseneath The property of L Wilson Esq
290	Glen Sannox, Arran – Clear Mid-day Effect

1834

EDINBURGH SA
Glasgow

4	Arran from Bute – Effect of Sunshine breaking through a Rainy Cloud The property of D C Rait Esq

70 Group of Trees, on the Cart
    The property of D Mackie Esq
123 Sketch of Mearns Moor
    The property of D Macnee Esq SA
165 Cruikstone Castle
175 Loch Lomond, near Luss
    The property of John Fleming Esq of Claremont
198 Drymen Moor, Effect of Storm

GLASGOW DS
Govanhaugh, Hutchesontown, Glasgow

27 Glen Sannox, Island of Arran
108 Cruikston Castle
113 Study of Trees
115 Clyde, from the Hills above Erskine Ferry
125 Dalmally, with the Hills of Glenorchy in the distance
131 Carbeth House
147 Group of Trees on the Cart
158 Distant View of the Lake of Menteith
163 Scene on the Old Road, near Moffat
252 Sunset
262 Moor Scene, near Kilbride

MANCHESTER RMI

187 Moor Scene, near the Battleground of Drumclog, Stormy effect

1835

EDINBURGH SA
Glasgow

75 Campsie Glen — Sunset
    The property of D Macnee Esq SA
80 Sketch in Cadzow Park
88 View in Cadzow Park, near Hamilton, part of the ancient Caledonian Forest
102 Druidical Stones, Island of Arran — Moonlight
    The property of J Westwater Esq
109 View from the Roman Camp at Dalzell, near Hamilton
128 The Head of Loch Awe
156 Glen Rosa, Island of Arran
221 Moor Scene

GLASGOW DS
Govanhaugh, Hutchesontown, Glasgow

18 A waterfall in the Rooking Glen
69 View of Eastwood — painted for Mrs Robert Thomson, Southfield
109 Highland Glen — early morning — a sketch for a large picture
139 Old Bridge over the Avon, near Hamilton

MANCHESTER RMI
473 Buchanan St, Glasgow

98 Glen Rosa, Isle of Arran
106 Landscape . . . Scotland
211 Druidical Stones, Island of Arran — Moonlight

1836

EDINBURGH SA
Glasgow

4 A Scottish strath
14 Loch Goil
    The property of Dr James Brown Glasgow
50 Loch Eck
136 Sunset
140 Moor Scene

GLASGOW DS

No exhibits

LIVERPOOL LA
Glasgow

294 Twilight
434 Moor Scene

MANCHESTER RMI
71 Buchanan St, Glasgow*

73 Scene on the Coast, Renfrewshire
406 Druidical Stones, Kintyre

*The address of Archibald Brodie, carver and gilder

1837

EDINBURGH SA
Hamilton

27 Loch-an-Elin, with the stronghold of the Wolf of Badenoch
60 A Highland Loch
72 Druidical Stones in Kintyre
114 View near Aberfoyle
167 Kilchurn Castle, Loch Awe, Showery effect
    The property of Daniel Macnee Esq SA
189 Glen in Badenoch with the remains of the old Pine Forest — Sunset

GLASGOW DS

No exhibits

1838

EDINBURGH SA
Hamilton

23 Hardyknute's Castle, Renfrewshire
    The property of Alex S Logan Esq Advocate
51 Cadzow Castle

57 Dunderawe Castle, Loch Fine
73 View in Cadzow Forest
129 Sunset
190 Bothwell Castle — a Day in June
210 Loch-An-eilin Inverness-shire with part of the Pine Forest
238 Kilchurn Castle, Loch Awe — Breezy effect
309 View of Castle Semple and Lake
The property of Colonel Harvey, of Castle Semple

GLASGOW DS

No exhibits

NEWCASTLE NES

89 Cadrew Castle, on the River Avon, Lanarkshire — June Day effect

1839

EDINBURGH RSA

12 Howard Place, Edinburgh

35 Moonlight
80 Cottages in Strathaven
90 Govan, on the Clyde
165 Castle Campbell
'The Castle of Gloom in the Vale of Sorrow'
212 A Forest Glade
The property of D O Hill Esq RSA
234 A Highland Loch
272 Cathcart Castle — Sunset
320 A Muir Scene
409 A Highland Road Scene

GLASGOW

No exhibition

1840

EDINBURGH RSA

12 Howard Place, Edinburgh

46 A Highland Solitude, with Druidical Stones
83 Edinburgh, from Corstorphine Hill — Effect after Rain
152 A Highland Scene — Approaching Twilight
'Now fades the glimmering landscape on the sight'
[Thomas Gray]
219 Goodriche Court and Castle, on the River Wye
263 Highland Lake Scene
279 Moonlight — Deer Startled
296 Sunset

GLASGOW

No exhibition

1841

EDINBURGH RSA

12 Howard Place, Edinburgh

9 View on the Coast of Ayrshire
21 Glen Messen, Argyleshire
'The land where the clouds love to rest,
like the sheet of the dead, on the mountain's cold breast'
[Mrs Robinson]
130 Cambuskenneth Abbey on the Forth — Moonlight
'The moon is up, but yet it is not night'
Byron
272 Moor Scene — Sunset
410 Highland Loch — Morning

GLASGOW WSA

Edinburgh

69 Landscape
182 Landscape

1842

BELFAST NIAU

27 Scene in the Island of Arran

EDINBURGH RSA

12 Howard Place, Edinburgh

113 A Road Scene on the Banks of Loch Long — the Arrochar Hills in distance
210 The Last Gleam of Light — Highland Landscape
'The fading beams of the descending sun
Still wandered over all the western sky,
Touching each mountain top and passing cloud,
While all below was shadow, thought and silence'.
263 A Highland Scene — Rainy Effect
320 Arran seen from Ettrick Bay, Island of Bute

GLASGOW WSA

12 Howard Place, Edinburgh

25 Newark Castle
39 Moonlight
52 Sunset on the Clyde

LIVERPOOL LA

12 Howard Place, Edinburgh

266 Moor Scene — Scotland — Effect — Rain passing off

1843

DUBLIN RHA

12 Howard Place, Edinburgh

52 Distant view of the island of Arran, from Bute
192 Scene in Cadzow Forest, near Hamilton

EDINBURGH RSA
12 Howard Place, Edinburgh

36   Loch Katrine, from the Boat House
53   Ben Venue and part of the Trossachs
422   Near Kilmun — Effect of Rain passing off
437   Scene in Cadzow Forest — Evening

GLASGOW WSA
14* Howard Place, Edinburgh

27   Highland Solitude — Moon Rising
208   Scene in Cadzow Forest, near Hamilton
247   Ben-Venue — Twilight Effect

*Presumably a mistake in the original catalogue

LONDON RA
12 Howard Place, Edinburgh

66   Old bridge over the Avon, near Hamilton
289   Scene in Cadrew Forest

NEWCASTLE NES

29   Loch Fad Island of Bute, the mountains of Arran in the distance

1844

DUBLIN RHA
12 Howard Place, Edinburgh

125   Highland Scene, near Loch Levin, Argyleshire, Druidical Stones in the foreground effect — rain passing off

EDINBURGH RSA
12 Howard Place, Edinburgh

38   View of Loch Fad, Isle of Bute — Arran in the distance
150   Highland Pass — Stormy Effect
156   Moonlight
174   Loch Ard — Sunset
227   A Dream of the Highlands
318   Kilchurn Castle
453   Limekiln, West Highlands

GLASGOW WSA
12 Howard Place, Edinburgh

29   Study of an Effect seen on the Avondhu — Benlomond in the Distance
56   Bridle Path in the Marquis of Breadalbane's Deer-Forest, Black Mount, Argyllshire

1845

DUBLIN RHA
12 Howard Place, Edinburgh

205   Moreland — Scene near Stirling, Scotland

EDINBURGH RSA
12 Howard Place, Edinburgh

40   On the Avendhu — Benlomond in the distance
41   Scene in the Marquis of Breadalbane's Deer Forest — Twilight Effect
     The property of William Dennistoun Esq, Glasgow
51   Ballachulish on Loch Leven
     The property of William Dennistoun Esq
117   Twilight Effect
227   Glencoe
342   Invercoe — the scene of the Massacre of Glencoe

GLASGOW WSA
12 Howard Place, Edinburgh

36   Ballahulish on Loch-Leven, Argyleshire
49   Scene near Loch-Etive, Argyleshire
84   Glencoe
     The property of William Denniston Esq
184   Moor-Scene in the Black Mount, Argyleshire
     The property of William Denniston Esq
221   Sunset in the Marquis of Breadalbane's Deer Forest
     The property of William Denniston Esq

1846

CARLISLE
12 Howard Place, Edinburgh

1   Highland Landscape — The Last Gleam

EDINBURGH RSA
12 Howard Place, Edinburgh

58   Highland Landscape
218   Druidical Stones, Isle of Arran
296   Bothwell Castle, River Clyde
     The property of Charles Finlay Esq
361   Moonlight

GLASGOW WSA
12 Howard Place, Edinburgh

74   Moorland Scene, near Stirling
92   Twilight Effect, Pass of Killicrankie
     The property of Charles Hutchins Esq
122   View of Stirling Castle, from the Field of Bannockburn
161   Highland Peat Moss
171   Loch Doon Castle, Ayrshire

MANCHESTER RMI
12 Howard Place, Edinburgh

612   Moor Scene in the West Highlands

1847

EDINBURGH RSA
12 Howard Place, Edinburgh

70 Highland Peat-Moss, Lochaber
102 Scene in the Marquis of Breadalbane's Deer Forest, Black Mount, Argyleshire
  The property of the Marquis of Breadalbane
119 Moor Scene
202 Loch-Doon Castle
230 Misty Corries — Haunts of the Red Deer
  Sold to Mr Alexander Hill, Publisher to HER MAJESTY and to the Royal Scottish Academy, Prince's Street, Edinburgh
278 The Ardgour Mountains, from Ballahulish — Sunset
372 Inversnaid Ferry, Loch Lomond
  The property of Thomas Brown Esq, Glasgow

GLASGOW WSA
12 Howard Place, Edinburgh

19 Moonlight
192 Highland Landscape, Dunstaffnage Castle
  The property of James Walker Esq, Edinburgh

MANCHESTER RMI

44 Highland Strath

1848

EDINBURGH RSA
12 Howard Place, Edinburgh

23 Dunsquaich Castle — Ancient stronghold of the Macdonalds of Sleate
157 Moonlight
298 The Range of the Cullin Mountains, from Gillian Bay, Isle of Skye
  The property of William Dennistoun Esq
393 Blavin, the highest Mountain in Skye
  'Thy matchless grandeur now no cloudlet veils,
  With mystic fold, thy dark bewildering form,
  Thy confines grim, where howls the frequent storm;
  Proud Blavin! frown not as the calm prevails,
  Majestic thou when wrack thy tower assails;
  Spurn not reproachful the alluring smile,
  Whose charms thy mists brief space from thrall beguile;
  Rude joy is thine, as wild Atlantic wails.
  Ah! summon not, mid glowing firmament,
  Thy warriors stern to find thy battlement;
  They slumber fitful in their sullen cave:
  Forth will they rush to quell the rising wave;
  Glad ocean greeteth thy unveiled head,
  Thus in his tranquil mirror welcomed.'
  Gleams of Thought, by Lord Robertson
467 Loch Corrisk, Isle of Skye
  The property of William Dennistoun Esq, Glasgow

GLASGOW WSA
21 Howard Place, Edinburgh

41 Loch Corrisk, Isle of Skye
  The property of William Dennistoun Esq, Glasgow
90 Range of the Coolin Mountains, from Gillian Bay, Isle of Skye
  The property of William Dennistoun Esq, Glasgow
155 A View of the Coast of Sleate, Isle of Skye

LIVERPOOL LA
21 Howard Place, Edinburgh

71 Scene in the Duke of Montrose's Deer Forest, Loch Lomond

LONDON BI
Edinburgh & 5 Haymarket, London

277 Glencoe 4'2 × 5'8 [frame size]

LONDON FE
13 Howard Place, Edinburgh

312 Misty Corries — Haunts of the Red Deer £200

1849

EDINBURGH RSA
21 Howard Place, Edinburgh

36 A Highland Stronghold
  'All ruined and wild is their roofless abode,
  And lonely the dark raven's sheltering tree;
  And travell'd by few is the grass covered road,
  Where the Hunter of deer and the warrior trode,
  To his hills that encircle the sea.'
  Campbell
85 Scene on the Island of Inch Murran, Loch Lomond
282 View of Loch Lomond
  The property of William Wilson Esq of Bank Knock
316 Scavig, Isle of Skye
454 Landscape [in West Room: watercolours miniatures etc]

GLASGOW WSA
54 Inverleith Row, Edinburgh

180 Highland Landscape, Sunset

LONDON FE
Howard Street, Edinburgh

308 A Highland Stronghold £200

1850

EDINBURGH RSA
54 Inverleith Row, Edinburgh

43 Lime kiln in the Highlands

144 A Quiet River
194 Scene on the West Coast of Scotland
     The property of JOHN MILLER Esq of Liverpool
214 A Forest Glade

GLASGOW WSA
54 Inverleith Row, Edinburgh

49 Loch Ard, Sunset
82 A Lime-Kiln in the Highlands

LONDON NI
54 Inverleith Row, Edinburgh

298 Border Tower on the Yarrow £63

1851

EDINBURGH RSA
54 Inverleith Row, Edinburgh

91 'Lowland River' — Sunset
172 Sunset
     The property of Mr JAMES KEITH, PRINCE'S STREET
231 A Highland Peat Moss
     The property of CHARLES BLACK Esq
350 In the Sound of Mull

GLASGOW WSA

No exhibits

LONDON NI

No address given

18 Lime Kiln in the Highlands £84

1852

EDINBURGH RSA
54 Inverleith Row, Edinburgh

65 Loch Coriskin, Isle of Skye
    No marvel thus the monarch spake;
      For rarely human eye has known
    A scene so stern as that dread lake,
      With its dark ledge of barren stone.
    Seems that primeval earthquake's sway
    Hath rent a strange and shatter'd way
      Through the rude bosom of the hill,
    And that each naked precipice,
    Sable ravine and dark abyss
      Tells of the outrage still.

    And wilder forward as they wound
    Were the proud cliffs and lake profound.
    Huge terraces of granite black
    Afforded rude and cumber'd track;
      For from the mountain hoar,
    Hurl'd headlong in some night of fear,

    When yell'd the wolf and fled the deer,
      Loose crags had toppled o'er;
    And some, chance poised and balanced, lay,
    So that a stripling arm might sway
      A mass no host could raise,
    In Nature's rage at random thrown
    Yet trembling like the Druid's stone,
    On its precarious base.
      Vide The Lord of the Isles [Sir Walter Scott]
100 A Bit of Woodland
230 The Drove Road

GLASGOW WSA
7 Henderson Row, Edinburgh

193 Lowland River, Autumn Evening, Sunset
     The property of Robert Cox Esq W S, Edinburgh
284 Glencoe, looking down, mist rising after rain
326 Loch Coriskin, Isle of Skye

1853

EDINBURGH RSA
7 Henderson Row, Edinburgh

155 Glencoe looking down the Glen — Effect of Mist
     rising after Rain
219 Edinburgh from Spylaw — Autumn Afternoon
400 A Sunset
518 Landscape Thoughts
519 Landscape Thoughts
543 Drawing in Black
544 Drawing in Black
659 Drawing in Black
660 Drawing in Black

GLASGOW WSA
7 Henderson Row, Edinburgh

54 View of Loch Eck
     The property of Thomas Auchterlonie, Esq
145 Tower of Glen Dearg
     The property of James Rodger Esq
278 The Arrochar Mountains from Inversnaid Ferry
     The property of Thomas Brown Esq

1854

EDINBURGH RSA
7 Henderson Row, Edinburgh

76 Caisteal Chaoil-Chuirn, Loch Awe
238 The Coolin Mountains, Isle of Skye
361 The Edge of a Wood — sunset

GLASGOW

No further exhibitions until 1861

1855

EDINBURGH RSA

7 Danube Street, Edinburgh

13 Knock Castle and the Sound of Sleat, Isle of Skye
76 A Carpenter's Shop in the village of Currie near
    Edinburgh, painted on the spot
158 Dunstaffnage Castle, Argyleshire
    The property of D Hutcheson Esq, Glasgow
178 Sunset
272 The Frith of Forth and Edinburgh from Dalmeny Park
508 Old Highland Mill, Morven, Argyleshire — painted on
    the spot
727 Old Houses at Oban, Argyleshire, painted on the spot
    [in Watercolour Room]

1856

EDINBURGH RSA

7 Danube Street, Edinburgh

59 Storm on a Highland Coast, Isle of Skye
85 Autumn — Sunset
112 Loch Ard — Sunset
    The property of John Wilson Esq, Glasgow
207 Highland Deer Forest, Isle of Skye
    'Land of brown heath and shaggy wood
    Land of the Mountain and the flood'
                              [Sir Walter Scott]
367 The Dean Castle, near Kilmarnock
431 The Lynn Spout, Dalry, Ayrshire

1857

EDINBURGH RSA

7 Danube Street, Edinburgh

79 Inverlochy Castle
114 Loch-Aline Castle, Sound of Mull
150 Summer-day in Skye — View of the Cullin Mountains
316 Mill on the River Irvine, Ayrshire
    The property of John Houldsworth Esq, Glasgow

MANCHESTER AT

463 Loch Awe
    Lent by C D Young

1858

EDINBURGH RSA

7 Danube Street, Edinburgh

157 Moon rising in a Highland Glen — Autumn
244 Highlander's Shieling on the side of Benlomond
    The property of Professor Simpson

265 Morning
    The property of Robert Horn Esq
269 Evening
    The property of Robert Horn Esq
330 Sunshine among Showers

1859

EDINBURGH RSA

7 Danube Street, Edinburgh

90 Peat Moss on Loch Shiel, Inverness-shire
    The property of Wynn Williams Esq, London
111 Moonlight
133 Sunset on a Scottish River
    The property of Allan Gilmour Esq, Eaglesham
162 The Clyde from Dalnotter Hill
    The property of James Tennant Caird Esq, of
    Greenock. To be engraved in line in the best manner
    by William Forrest Edinburgh
397 Limekiln on the Banks of Loch Shiel, Inverness-shire

1860

EDINBURGH RSA

7 Danube Street, Edinburgh

301 Loch Achray and the Trossachs
    The property of Matthew M Muir Esq
358 Study of Trees at Gair Loch, Ross-shire, painted on
    the spot
373 Castle Turim, the stronghold of the Clan Ranolds
    'All ruin'd and wild is their roofless abode
    And lonely the dark raven's sheltering tree;
    and travell'd by few is the grass-covered road,
    Where the hunter of deer and the warrior trod
    To his hills that encircle the sea'   Campbell
517 Druidical Stones — Moonlight

1861

EDINBURGH RSA

7 Danube Street, Edinburgh

145 Evening — Diploma Picture — Painted for the Royal
    Scottish Academy
289 Mist rising off Mountains
    The property of James Lumsden Esq, Glasgow
408 Sea-Beach on the Coast of Ayr

GLASGOW GIFA

7 Danube Street, Edinburgh

40 River Scene — Sunset
67 Morning on a Highland Loch
    'For yet the sun was wading through the mist'
                              [Allan Ramsay]

217 Autumn — Moon-rise in a Highland Glen £262*
283 Loch Achray
437 Lord Macdonald's Deer Forest, Isle of Skye

*Price scored out in GAG copy of catalogue and replaced by
'Property of Jas Rogers' (in pencil) and 'Rodgers' (in ink)

1862

EDINBURGH RSA
7 Danube Street, Edinburgh

102 A Highland Loch — Morning
'As yet the sun was wading through the mist'
[Allan Ramsay]
276 The Moss — Loch Shiel, Inverness-shire
376 Ben Venue — Loch Katrine, from near the Silver
Strand
440 River Scene — Sunset
The property of J C Bell Esq, Broughty Ferry
578 River Scene — Sunset
597 The Island of Mull, from Karrara, near Oban,
Argyleshire — Sunset

GLASGOW GIFA
Edinburgh

72 Loch Katrine, from the Silver Strand
The property of Sir Andrew Orr
185 Bridge of the Three Waters, Glencoe
The property of David Hutchison Esq
405 Light House — Stormy Effect
413 Sound of Kerraro

LIVERPOOL LA
7 Danube Street, Edinburgh

191 Hivercoe the scene of the Massacre of Glencoe

LONDON IE

626 Druidical Stones, Moonlight
Lent by A O Ewing
706 Loch Achray
Lent by M A Muir

1863

EDINBURGH RSA
St Colm, Trinity, Edinburgh

171 Highland Mill
The property of J Charles Bell Esq
232 Moonlight
The property of Dr Malcolm, Edinburgh
319 Glencoe, from the Bridge of Three Waters
The property of D Hutcheson Esq
450 Highland Lime-kiln
512 Bothwell Castle, on the Clyde

EDINBURGH RSA (loan exh October)
No address given

36 Loch Corriskin Skye
Lent by Alex Macdonald
47 Loch Katrine, from the Silver Strand
Lent by Sir Andrew Orr
159 Deer Forest, Sligichan Skye
'Land of brown heath and shaggy wood
Land of the mountain and the flood'
[Sir Walter Scott]
Lent by David Richardson Esq, Glasgow
205 Landscape — Muir Scene
Lent by J T Gibson-Craig Esq

GLASGOW GIFA
St Colm, Trinity, Edinburgh

46 Castle Kilchurn, Loch Awe
The property of Daniel Macnee Esq
206 Loch Lomond
373 Glencoe — Mist rising after Rain
The property of A G Macdonald Esq

1864

DUBLIN RHA
No address given

305 On the River Dee
The property of J A Aitken Esq

EDINBURGH RSA
St Colm, Trinity, Edinburgh

231 Sundown — Loch Achray
The property of James Patrick Esq, Benmore,
Argyleshire
380 Kilchurn Castle, Loch Awe
The property of Daniel Macnee Esq RSA
484 Mill in Glenfinlas — painted on the spot
489 Sun rising through a mist
The property of David L Gibson Esq
602 M'Farlane's Island, Loch Lomond — Moonlight

GLASGOW
No exhibition

1865

EDINBURGH RSA
St Colm, Trinity, Edinburgh

8 Sketch — Tinker's Camp
146 Group of Trees
The property of J Mackenzie Esq
155 Highland Road scene
218 Dunskiach Castle, Isle of Skye

307 An Old Oak in Cadzow Forest
'whose boughs are mossed with age
And high top bald with dry antiquity'
As You Like It [Shakespeare]

425 Glencoe
The property of James Patrick Esq of Kilmun

669 Loch Achray
The property of James Patrick Esq of Kilmun

815 Sunset
The property of Thomas Chapman Esq

GLASGOW GIFA
St Colm, Trinity, Edinburgh

16 Loch Achray
The property of D R Hay Esq, Edinburgh

187 Head of Loch-Fyne
The property of John Mathieson Jun Esq

1866

DUBLIN RHA
No address given

33 Roslin Castle
The property of J Aitken Esq

102 The Smugglers Cove, Coast of Sollway
The property of J Aitken Esq

166 Entrance to Glenlyon
The property of J Aitken Esq

EDINBURGH RSA
St Colm, Trinity, Edinburgh

3 The Edge of a Wood

8 Sundown in a Highland Glen

132 In the Wood

453 Loch Katrine
The property of William Harrison Esq

GLASGOW GIFA
St Colm, Trinity, Edinburgh

19 Mist Rising off Mountains
The property of James Lumsden Esq

1867

EDINBURGH RSA
St Colm, Trinity, Edinburgh

338 In the West Highlands
'All ruined and wild is their roofless abode,
And lonely the dark raven's sheltering tree,
And Travelled by few is the grass-covered road
Where the hunter of deer and the warrior trode
To his hills that encircle the sea'
[Thomas Campbell]

391 Loch Maree, Ross-shire
The property of David Hutcheson Esq

411 Glen Finnan — painted on the spot

EDINBURGH CLARK EXH (see p 7)

GLASGOW GIFA
St Colm, Trinity, Edinburgh

14 On the Marnock, Ayrshire
The property of PETER COATS Esq, Paisley

173 'My Heart's in the Highlands'
The property of DAVID HUTCHISON Esq

PARIS UE

Loch Katrine Perthshire
The property of William Harrison Esq

1868

DUBLIN RHA

292 Sketch on the Forth
The property of J A Aitken Esq

EDINBURGH RSA

558 Moonlight — unfinished (the last picture he touched;
he worked on it two days previous to his death)

612 A Sunset. Painted in 1867
The property of D L Gibson Esq

GLASGOW GIFA

21 The Lowland River
The property of Robert Cox Esq, Edinburgh

321 Loch-Maree (the Artist's last great work)
The property of David Hutchison Esq

NOTES ON CATALOGUE ENTRIES

The exhibits are catalogued in a more or less chronological sequence. Strict chronology has been abandoned in the case of studies (which come after the finished version) and closely related works (eg engravings). Undated works on paper are catalogued in groups with the same provenance or of approximately the same date.

Title: where possible the title given to the picture by the artist has been taken from the earliest exhibition record or from the artist's Account Book or other contemporary source. When no contemporary title is known, the title provided by the present owner, or the most accurate descriptive title is used.

Size: given in centimetres followed by inches in brackets, height before width.

Signature, date and other inscriptions: form and punctuation is facsimile. The colour is described only when more than one colour was used.

Provenance and *Exhibitions:* because very few of McCulloch's works can be traced back without interruption to their first owner or first public exhibition it has often been necessary to question the information in these sections even when there seems little doubt of its being correct.

   Additional information about previous owners and donors may be found in the index to previous collections p 107. For list of EXHIBITED WORKS 1828-68 see p 31.

References: some frequently recurring printed sources are referred to in abbreviated form. For full details see Bibliographical Abbreviations p 6.

Frames: where available, details of framemaker's labels are included as a note to the Provenance. An index of these framemakers is on p 106.

Black and white illustrations: where appropriate full details are given on p 110.

1

Reproduction in G Eyre Todd's
History of Glasgow 1934

Lithograph by David Allan
after McCulloch 1835

GLASGOW CATHEDRAL FROM DRYGATE   *c*1830

oil on panel

33.7 × 25.8 (13¼ × 10⅛)

inscribed *verso* (in pencil) *H McCulloch* and *No 21*

lent by Charles MacStravick

Prov: Purchased from Gordon Ingles, Springburn
*c*1960 by present owner

Exh: Possibly 1830 Glasgow DS (164) *High Church,
Glasgow, from Duke-Street*

McCulloch painted at least two, and probably three, versions of this subject. This may be the earliest and therefore his 1830 DS exhibit. It shows the late 12th century cathedral as it was before the towers were demolished in 1843. A second version was lithographed by David Allan for *Views in Glasgow and Neighbourhood* published by Allan and Ferguson in 1835 (see illus) and was perhaps the picture later owned by D S Cargill[1]. A similar view, but different in detail from both the present work and the Allan lithograph, was illustrated in G Eyre Todd's *History of Glasgow* 1934 vol 3 attributed in the caption to McCulloch and said to be dated 1832. The owner was not given and its present whereabouts is not known (see illus).

   Painted soon after the artist returned to Glasgow from Edinburgh (see p 12) this small oil shows that McCulloch has already moved away from the neatly presented, busy detail of a Knox street scene. The dramatic effect of stormy lighting on a familiar cityscape takes precedence over careful architectural recording.

1   *Glasgow Cathedral from the Drygate 1834* included in the 1867 Edinburgh Clark Exh (82) lent by D S Cargill, and again in the 1901 Glasgow *International Exhibition* (1919) *The Drygate with Cathedral* where it is claimed in the catalogue to be McCulloch's DS exhibit. (See also William Young 'The Glasgow Exhibition . . .' *Glasgow Herald* 24 July 1901.)

2

LANDSCAPE COMPOSITION   1830

pen and brown ink, wash and pencil on cream-coloured wove paper pasted on card

13.9 × 23.4 (5½ × 9³⁄₁₆)

signed and dated lower right (in brown ink)
H. McCulloch/1830 and (in another style)
composition by/Horatio McCulloch, inscribed *verso*
(in pencil) *Presented to Robert Maxwell Esq/of
Maxwellton Place Paisley Rd/Glasgow/1830 by
Horiato* [sic] *McCulloch/his Dear Friend*

lent by Glasgow Art Gallery and Museum

Prov: Purchased from John C Hall 1924 (*24-28*)

This is the earliest known dated work by McCulloch and was given by him to his Glasgow friend the amateur painter Robert Maxwell (dates unknown). McCulloch and Maxwell were amongst a group of artists and intellectuals who frequented Bellfield Cottage, the Kirkintilloch home of William Thomson (*c*1777-1853), in the early 1830s (see also Cat No 7). Maxwell was described by James Hedderwick[1] as '. . . an amateur in still life, but leading a life the reverse of still . . . Maxwell in particular had mimical and musical gifts which rendered his society something to be coveted . . .' Along with McCulloch and their friend the animal painter John Sheriff (1816-44), Maxwell was caught up in the 1835 pamphlet controversy which resulted in McCulloch's rift with the Glasgow Dilettanti Society (see p 15-16).

1   *Backward Glances* Edinburgh and London   1891

3

BOWLING   *c*1830-5

oil on canvas[1]

81.3 × 127 (32 × 50)

lent by Glasgow Art Gallery and Museum

Prov: Mary A C Maxwell Bequest 1932   *Reg No 1834*

Exh: Possibly 1832 Glasgow DS (3) *Clyde, from Dunnotter Hill*; 1974 Knox Exh (33) as by unknown artist

Ref: Donnelly p 9 pl 10

Engraving after McCulloch in Lumsden's *Steam-Boat Companion* 1831

John Knox FIRST STEAMBOAT ON THE CLYDE *c*1830

Engraving after McCulloch in Beattie's *Scotland* 1838

When this picture was shown in the 1974 Knox Exhibition its McCulloch attribution was doubted, but with the qualification 'unless it is an extremely early work'. Since 1974 a number of McCulloch's early works have come to light and stylistic comparison, backed by scientific analysis, now indicates a reasonably certain McCulloch attribution for this painting.

Its subject, the Clyde from Dalnottar Hill[2], was in the early 19th century one of the most frequently depicted locations in the West of Scotland. The view is described in Lumsden's *Steam-Boat Companion* 1831 thus: 'Here suddenly bursts upon the sight, one of the most admirable prospects perhaps in the world. In front, the Clyde expands to a noble breadth, bounded on the north by the steep and wooded hills of Kilpatrick, and on the south by the sloping hills of Renfrewshire; while the castles of Dunglass and Dunbarton jutting into the river, with the lofty mountains of Argyle in the distance, give a finishing to a picture, which, for richness and variety, is rarely to be contemplated.' The view is now partially obscured by the Erskine Bridge and other 20th century developments.

McCulloch would have known Alexander Nasmyth's famous Clyde-view drop-curtain at Glasgow's Theatre Royal (see p 10), which was destroyed in a disastrous fire in January 1829. He would also have seen and possibly assisted with some of the many versions of this view produced by the Glasgow landscape painter, John Knox[3], and McCulloch himself had already depicted it before this present version was painted. His very first exhibit with the SA, in 1829, was *View on the Clyde* which was probably the picture now known only through an engraving in Lumsden's *Steam-Boat Companion* (see illus). The composition follows the traditional Claudian formula favoured by Nasmyth and Knox: trees frame the scene and direct the eye along the winding river to Dumbarton Rock in the distance[4]. In *Bowling* the artist has abandoned this formula, along with the overall minute attention to detail which characterises the Knox renderings of the view (see illus). Here the background hills dissolve into the sky, the middle distance is broadly brushed in whilst carefully drawn detail is confined to the foreground.

In Cat No 44 painted more than twenty years later, McCulloch has reverted to a more conventional composition, perhaps to satisfy the conservative taste of his patron.

1 For technical report see p 103
2 Variations in the spelling include Dalnotter, Dunotter
3 For a discussion of McCulloch's relationship to Knox see p 9-10
4 The engraving after McCulloch *The Clyde, with Dunbarton Castle in the Distance* in W Beattie's *Scotland* (1838) also follows the traditional pattern (see illus)

4

THE CLYDE NEAR DUMBARTON   *c*1830-5

oil on slate

90 × 75 (35 × 30½)

lent by the McLean Museum and Art Gallery, Greenock

Prov: Presented by Mr Berkeley Robertson, Glasgow
1953   *Reg No A162*

Ref: Donnelly p 9

Exh: 1987 Greenock McLean Museum and Art Gallery
Best of the McLean

A more distant view than the popular one (see previous entry), in this painting the artist's main interest is in atmospheric effects, although the spindly tree on the left is a concession to the classical tradition.

Why McCulloch came to use such an unusual support for this painting — a quite thick, and consequently heavy, slab of slate — is uncertain. A possible explanation is that it was part of an interior decorative scheme, perhaps for a fireplace surround. This might also account for the slightly uncomfortable choice of an upright format for an essentially horizontal subject. On the other hand he may have simply chosen slate as an experimental surface.

5

ST BLANE'S CHURCH BUTE   *c*1830-3

oil over pencil on panel

18.4 × 34.4 (7¼ × 13⁹⁄₁₆)

signed lower right *H McCulloch*

lent by Bute Museum

Prov: Transferred to Bute Museum from the RSM
*c*1950

McCulloch's first visit to the island of Bute, in the Firth
of Clyde, took place sometime before the Glasgow
Dilettanti Society's autumn 1831 exhibition in which he
showed (304) *View of Arran from Bute,* two Loch Fad
subjects (176) and (330) and (316) *Sketch, – near
Rothsay* [sic]. He exhibited further Bute subjects in
1833 and 1834 and again in the 1840s, although the
latter may have been done from earlier studies. The
present small oil may therefore date from as early as
1830 or 1831, and was probably done on-the-spot.

The ruin of St Blane's Church is at the southern end
of the island in a valley above Dunagoil Bay. In the
painting the hills of Arran can be seen across the water
beyond the screen of trees. According to Dorothy
Marshall 'The present ruin dates from the 12th Century,
when it was a two-chamber church with the lovely
Norman arch dividing the chancel from the nave. It
appears to have been extended eastward during the
next century. The lower wall of the extension is of
rubble and some of the Norman masonry has been re-
used above this. In the 14th or 15th Century the
chancel windows were altered, the remains of the
earlier one being visible before the later, two-light one.
About that time the nave was extended to the west.
Until the Reformation, St Blane's came under the
jurisdiction of Paisley Abbey. Right on to the beginning
of the 18th Century, this church was used for regular
worship'[1].

1 Dorothy N Marshall *History of Bute* Bute Museum, 7th ed
   1978 (revised 1981) p 41

6

SUMMER DAY ARRAN   *c*1833

oil on prepared board[1]

24.2 × 34.9 (9½ × 13¾)

signed lower left (in brown) *H.McCulloch*:
inscribed lower centre (in black) *Summer Day Arran* [?] *H . . .* (illegible)

lent by Martyn Gregory

Prov: With Daniel Shackleton Edinburgh 1986 from
.whom acquired by present owner

The inscription lower centre was smudged whilst the paint was still wet but the third word can be fairly confidently read as Arran. Although undated there is little doubt, for stylistic reasons, that this study was done during a visit to Arran early in the artist's career. Judging from exhibited titles a first visit took place in the summer of 1833 which resulted in three Arran subjects in that autumn's Dilettanti Society exhibition. Later Arran exhibits may derive from this one visit, or perhaps indicate further time spent on the island.

1   The support appears to be the cover of a sketch pad. A printed label *verso* (torn) reads 'A New Sketch Book . . . & Miller'

AN OPEN LANDSCAPE WITH TREES AND FIGURE ?1833

ink and watercolour on wove paper stuck down on card[1]

9.3 × 13.5 ($3\frac{5}{8}$ × $5\frac{5}{16}$)

lent by the Hunterian Art Gallery, University of Glasgow

Prov: Macgeorge Album; H Jefferson Barnes; purchased from him 1960   *(DW377)*

7

This drawing and Cat Nos 8-10 are from an album compiled by M Macgeorge in 1874. M Macgeorge is presumed to have been Margaret the wife of Andrew Macgeorge, the Glasgow lawyer, antiquarian and biographer of William Leighton Leitch, who in the 1830s, along with McCulloch, was one of the Bellfield Cottage circle (see entry for Cat No 2).

The album (part of which is still intact) contained a miscellany of drawings by such artists as Leitch, H W Williams and Andrew Donaldson. Each item was pasted down and titled on the mount in red ink with the artist's name and sometimes a date.

Fraser (p 23) records that Macgeorge acquired an album belonging to William Thomson of Bellfield '. . . A large album formed one of the usual attractions at Bellfield Cottage. To this all and sundry were invited to contribute. Eminent artists from a distance sometimes adorned the pages . . .' It has not been possible to determine whether the M Macgeorge album is an entirely separate creation or whether it was made up of items formerly in Thomson's album. Whichever is the case, the Macgeorge provenance adds authority to the inscribed attributions and dates. Comparison with the 1830 signed drawing Cat No 2 reinforces the Macgeorge evidence; the rather stylised trees in the 1830 drawing recur in the Macgeorge watercolours.

1   On which is written in red ink H McCULLOCH 1833

HIGHLAND LANDSCAPE WITH TWO FIGURES AND TWO DOGS   ?1833

watercolour with some scraping and wiping out on wove paper stuck down on card[1]

12.6 × 18.9 (5 × $7\frac{7}{16}$)

lent by the Hunterian Art Gallery, University of Glasgow

Prov: Macgeorge Album; H Jefferson Barnes; purchased from him 1960   *(DW378)*

8

McCulloch is said to have based his early watercolour style on that of H W Williams and to have copied the latter's work in Edinburgh in the mid 1820s (see p 11). Parallels with Williams are apparent in this particular watercolour: the forms of the leaves to the right of the picture and the method of wiping out to accentuate their shapes are Williams' mannerisms.

For a note on the provenance see entry for Cat No 7.

1   On which is written in red ink H McCULLOCH 1833

9

TREES AND WATERFALL ?1833

pencil and watercolour on white wove paper stuck down on card[1]

14×11 ($5\frac{1}{2} \times 4\frac{5}{16}$)

lent from a private collection

Prov: Macgeorge Album; H Jefferson Barnes by 1960

Exh: 1987 Glasgow Art Gallery *William Leighton Leitch*

For a note on the provenance see entry for Cat No 7.

1 On which is written in red ink *H McCULLOCH 1833*

10

A COW ?1835

pencil and watercolour on white wove paper stuck down on card[1]

10.4×13.2 ($4\frac{1}{16} \times 5\frac{1}{4}$)

lent from a private collection

Prov: Macgeorge Album; H Jefferson Barnes by 1960

The attribution of this drawing depends upon the reliability of the inscription on the mount, and the Macgeorge provenance (see entry for Cat No 7).

1 On which is written in red ink *H McCULLOCH/RECEIVED FROM HIMSELF 1835*

11

INVERARAY   1834

oil on panel

17.8 × 27.3 (7 × 10¾)

signed and dated lower right *H.McC 1834*

lent by Mr Joseph Brand, London

Prov¹: With Alastair Kerr, Inverbeg Galleries, Luss
   *c*1965; purchased from him by present owner

In this small sketch McCulloch focuses on the hill of
Duniquaich topped by its watch tower, the water of
Loch Fyne and Robert Mylne's two-arched bridge over
the River Aray. A hint of the elegant façade of Inveraray
New Town is seen to the left in the painting, but the
Duke of Argyll's celebrated castle is out of sight[2].
McCulloch had already produced a more conventional
view featuring the castle and fishing boats indicative of
the staple industry of the town, the herring fishery. This
was engraved for Lumsden's *Steam-Boat Companion*
(1831) and was probably McCulloch's 1831 SA exhibit
(329) *Inveraray Castle*.

   McCulloch most likely travelled to Loch Fyne
overland and by steamer via Loch Lomond in order to
produce the illustrations for Lumsden, perhaps in the
autumn of 1829 or sometime in 1830 (he showed Loch
Lomond subjects in Glasgow that autumn). The present
oil is evidence of a second visit, in 1834.

1   An old handwritten ink label on the back reads 'Inveraray
    by Horatio Mc[Culloch] Purchased in Edinburgh at Dow
    [?Dowells]'

2   For a detailed account of Inveraray see Ian G Lindsay and
    Mary Cosh, *Inveraray and the Dukes of Argyll*
    Edinburgh   1973

12

CADZOW FOREST   1834

oil over pencil on canvas[1]

42 × 68.6 (16½ × 27)

signed and dated lower right (in black) *H. M'Culloch . . . 1834* inscribed lower left (in greenish black) *Cadzow Forest painted on the spot.*

lent by James Lees-Milne

Prov: (?)Neale Thomson of Camphill; by descent to present owner

Exb: Possibly 1835 Edinburgh SA (80) *Sketch in Cadzow Park*[2]; 1986 Edinburgh and London *Painting in Scotland The Golden Age* (128) p 155

Ref: Possibly *Scotsman* 21 Feb 1835

Dated 1834, this small oil marks the beginning of McCulloch's fascination with the ancient oaks of Cadzow Forest. His obvious delight in a newly discovered sketching ground probably contributed to McCulloch's decision to settle in nearby Hamilton, sometime towards the end of 1835 (see p 16). He had exhibited two Cadzow subjects at the SA that spring, one of which may have been this picture, whilst the other earned him his Associateship[3]. A Cadzow engraving after McCulloch (see illus) was included in Beattie's *Scotland* (1838) and several oils of the forest survive which can be dated to c1835-8[4]. The most significant however, is at present untraced. It was one of his 1838 SA exhibits, (73) *View in Cadzow Forest* which, along with three other works, received effusive praise in the *Scotsman* (21 Feb): 'Noble is perhaps the proper term to apply to the picture of Cadzow Forest — its gnarled and antlered oaks, with its deep far-reaching glades . . .' The reviewer also draws attention to the wild white cattle which feature in most of McCulloch's Cadzow pictures, an ancient breed which was celebrated in verse by Sir Walter Scott[5] and which survives today[6].

    After his move to the capital in the late spring of 1838 McCulloch did not forget his favourite oak trees for they were the theme of an 1841 Glasgow exhibit and he chose to send a Cadzow subject to London in 1843 as one of his two first and only submissions to the Royal Academy exhibition (see p 21). An 1848

Horatio McCulloch CADZOW CASTLE *c*1835 (see note 4)

'composition' based on Cadzow was engraved by
William Forrest (see illus) and McCulloch sold several
small Cadzow subjects during the 1850s[7]. Later in life
he returned there to find distressing changes 'made by
time and "modern improvements", and the wanton
mischief of visitors'[8]. A favourite old oak had been
burnt down but he must have found an acceptable
substitute for one of his 1865 RSA exhibits was (307)
An Old Oak in Cadzow Forest[9].

CADZOW FOREST 1848 Engraving by William Forrest after
McCulloch (Fraser pl 2)

1   For technical report see p 103

2   Priced at £6 (annotated Exh Cat in RSA Library)

3   According to Fraser p 23. The SA minutes (RSA Library)
    record the election as taking place on 12 Nov 1834, before
    the picture was exhibited

4   eg Cat No 17; Sotheby's Glasgow 4 Feb 1987 lot 134 repr;
    Cadzow Castle (photo in file GAG Dept of Fine Art,
    unlocated oil)

5   'Cadyow [sic] Castle' in *Minstrelsy of the Scottish Border* pt
    III

6   *The White Cattle of Cadzow* Chatelherault Country Park
    MSC Programme 1986

7   Recorded in his Account Book

8   Fraser p 31

9   Purchased by RAPFAS £100 (Account Book May 1865)

13

VIEW FROM THE ROMAN CAMP AT DALZELL, NEAR HAMILTON 1835

oil on canvas[1]

56 × 76.2 (22 × 30)

signed and dated lower right *H McCulloch 1835.*

lent by Glasgow Art Gallery and Museum (The Hamilton Bequest)

Prov: (?) Sold to D R Hay 1835 25 gns[2]; with Mrs Robert Frank, London, 1952 as *Landscape* offered at £35[3]; acquired probably from her *c*1952 by Ray Livingston Murphy[4]; Murphy Estate sale Christie's 22 Nov 1985 lot 86 as *On the Tweed* purchased by the Trustees of the Hamilton Bequest *Reg No 3408*

Exh: (?)1835 Edinburgh SA (109) *View from the Roman Camp at Dalzell, near Hamilton*

Ref: *Glasgow Herald* 13 March 1835 (extract from *Edinburgh Evening Post* review of SA exhibition); Fraser p 23; Donnelly p 10

McCulloch's spacious prospect of the Clyde valley and Hamilton Palace was taken from an already well-established viewpoint at Dalzell just south of the present town of Motherwell. The view is now radically altered: a railway viaduct was constructed later in the 19th century, Hamilton Palace was demolished early this century and the M74 motorway bisects the scene. The artist's 1835 title *View from the Roman Camp at Dalzell* would however have immediately identified the location for a contemporary audience, for the place from which he had sketched the scene was at that time thought to be the site of a Roman camp (the modern town of Dalziell was yet to be built).

The parapet in the foreground belongs to a building known then as Archibald's Temple, which had been erected in 1736 by Archibald Hamilton (1694-1774) of Dalzell House[5]. Hamilton had discovered what he wrongly supposed to be the remains of a Roman site[6] and, inspired as well by the very splendid outlook, he built his Temple there and cleared the steep slope down to the river, planting trees and cutting terraced walks. In order to present the view as he did — it is a mid-summer or early autumn landsape — McCulloch must have visited the location before 1835 (the SA exhibition opened in February). The probable explanation is that he painted this canvas, or a version of it, during his 1834 visit to the Hamilton and Cadzow Forest area, adding the signature and date and perhaps some finishing touches before submitting the picture for exhibition at the Scottish Academy. It was praised in the Edinburgh press as 'remarkable for the beauty of its aerial perspective' which incidentally, may have been the quality which attracted the late owner, Ray Livingston Murphy, of whom it has been written 'Pictures of endless vistas fascinated Murphy'[7].

1   For technical report see p 103

2   Annotated SA Exh Cat (RSA Library)

3   NGS photo file

4   Murphy bought other items from Frank around this date (see catalogue of Christie's sale 22 Nov 1985)

5   Jack Sloan *Dalzell* Hamilton 1986 pp 32·5

6   Royal Commission on the Ancient and Historical Monuments of Scotland: *Lanarkshire, An Inventory of the Prebistoric and Roman Monuments* 1978 p 144

7   Catalogue of Christie's sale 22 Nov 1985 p 101

14

VIEW NEAR ABERFOYLE   1836

oil on panel

18.7×29.7 ($7\frac{3}{8} \times 11\frac{11}{16}$)

inscribed *verso* in ink *View near Aberfoyle/1836/ Horatio McCulloch*

lent from a private collection

Prov: (?)Acquired from the 1837 SA Exh by Sir George MacPherson Grant £10[1]; by descent to present owners

Exh: (?)1837 Edinburgh SA (114) *View near Aberfoyle*

Aberfoyle, a small village about 26 miles north of Glasgow *en route* to Loch Katrine and the Trossachs, features in Sir Walter Scott's *Rob Roy*

1   Price but no buyer's name given in annotated Exh Cat (RSA Library). There is however evidence in family sources that Sir George purchased works from SA exhibitions in both 1836 and 1838

15

BOTHWELL CASTLE   1837

oil on canvas

137 × 228.5 (54 × 90)

signed and dated lower left *H. McCulloch 1837*

lent from a private collection

Prov: Possibly commissioned by Alexander Logan in
            July 1837 (see below); Sotheby's, Central Hotel
            Glasgow 30 Nov 1976 lot 141 as *Log Cutters
            above a river*; Sotheby's Gleneagles 20 Aug
            1986 lot 593 as *Woodcutters, Bothwell Castle*[1];
            Andrew Whitfield, Calton Gallery, Edinburgh
            from whom acquired by present owner

Exh: Possibly 1838 Edinburgh SA (23) *Hardyknute's
            Castle, Renfrewshire* property of Alex S Logan
            Esq Advocate

Although it is not a faithful representation, the subject seems to be Bothwell Castle from the south-west looking towards the Clyde estuary in the far distance. McCulloch frequently strayed from topographical accuracy, especially it seems in paintings of Bothwell: 'In all his other pictures of Bothwell he had taken great liberties with the natural features of the place' (Fraser p 32).

McCulloch's first recorded Bothwell title was his 1831 DS exhibit (75), which was probably the original for the engraving in Lumsden's *Steam-Boat Companion* 1831 (see illus). It became one of his more frequent subjects until, according to Fraser, in 1862 he returned to Bothwell to spend six weeks making a preparatory study for a large painting, which was sold to Nathaniel Buckley of Ashton-Under-Lyme for £350 (Account Book). The present picture is dated 1837, and was painted whilst the artist was living at nearby Hamilton. Although he exhibited a Bothwell title in the 1838 SA Exh (190 *Bothwell Castle a Day in June*) this must have been a small painting, because it was purchased for only £35 by APFAS (large works by McCulloch were priced at around £150 at this date).

The explanation may be that the present painting was another 1838 exhibit, *Hardyknute's Castle, Renfrewshire* lent by Alexander Logan, a composition based on Bothwell Castle and that it was the picture mentioned by McCulloch in a letter to his friend J F Williams, dated 17 Nov 1837 (see p 18): 'I have painted a large picture for Logan. If you had time I wish you would go and see it his House is 12 Dublin Street'. This was Alexander Logan, an Edinburgh advocate, who had accompanied McCulloch on a visit to Hamilton Palace earlier that year, on 15 July[2]. Logan probably commissioned a picture on that occasion (the 1838 SA exhibit) and the present work is perhaps that picture[3].

If the above suggestions are correct, McCulloch's choice of Bothwell to represent Hardyknute's castle does not appear to have a precedent. The medieval castle of Bothwell has many historical and literary associations, but no reference to it as Hardyknute's castle has been traced. The historical Hardicanute was a cruel and despotic English king (1018-42); Hardyknute was the hero of a Scottish ballad attributed to Lady Elizabeth Wardlaw (1670-1727) and first published in 1719. The second verse contains the line 'Hie on a hill his castle stude'. Sir Walter Scott claimed that when a boy this was his favourite poem.

Engraving after McCulloch in Lumsden's *Steam-Boat Companion* 1831

1   Identified as Bothwell by Kitty Cruft in 1986

2   Hamilton Palace Visitors Book   (*GAG 23-44ad*)

3   There are no exhibition labels nor other indications of the painting's history other than a framemaker's label 'Bonnar & Carfrae, 77 George St, Edinburgh'

16

LANDSCAPE WITH WATERFALL *in situ* 1987

LANDSCAPE WITH WATERFALL   ?*c*1835-40

oil on canvas

284 × 152.4 (96 × 60)

lent by the Royal Scottish Academy of Music and Drama

Prov: Presented to the Glasgow Athenaeum by James Lumsden Esq of Yoker Lodge[1]; in the RSAMD building, St George's Place (renamed Nelson Mandela Place), until 1987 when RSAMD moved to new premises

16 The history of this painting remains a mystery despite a search[2] in the archives of both RSAMD and of its predecessor in the St George's Place building, the Glasgow Athenaeum.

A plaque recording its donation to the Athenaeum by James Lumsden of Yoker Lodge poses the question of whether this large work, which seems quite early in date, is one of the paintings commissioned by James Lumsden senior (see p 14) and referred to in 1872 by Fraser (p 20): '. . . the late Mr Lumsden, then Lord Provost of Glasgow . . . set him [McCulloch] to paint some large pictures for a public hall he had just built in St George's Place. These pictures still occupy their original places in what is now the public room of the Bedford Hotel[3]. They are of course totally wanting in any originality, but show a good eye for colour, great dexterity of hand and knowledge of effect . . .'.

More research might prove that the picture remained in Lumsden's 'public hall', which by 1872 had become the Bedford Hotel, until about 1888 when it was transferred to the Athenaeum's new building in St George's Place.

Both James Lumsdens were members of the Glasgow Athenaeum, a literary, commercial and scientific institution founded in 1847 and originally housed in the old Assembly Rooms, 110 Ingram Street[4]. By 1888 it would have been Lumsden junior who was involved in the inauguration of the Athenaeum's new premises[5].

He perhaps offered the painting at the planning stage of the new building for it was incorporated into the interior design of the concert hall by means of a decorative architectural surround (see illus). Whatever its early history, the Lumsden provenance supports the attribution to McCulloch, and comparison with a dated work such as Cat No 15 suggests a date of *c*1835-40[6]. Both paintings display the influence of the kind of wooded landscape produced by Rev John Thomson (see p 11) of which *Glen of Altnarie* (illus p 13) is a typical example.

17

THE BLASTED TREE   *c*1838

oil on canvas

76.3 × 54.7 (30 × 21¾)

signed lower left *H McCulloch RSA*

lent by Dundee Art Galleries and Museums (Orchar Collection)

Prov: Mrs G Anderson Craig; presented to the Orchar Collection, Broughty Ferry, 1967   *(393)*

Ref: James Morrison 'Horatio McCulloch — Painter of the Highland Landscape' *Seer* June 1980 repr p 15.

The artist's interest in specific trees is well illustrated here in his choice of an upright format for this portrait of a stricken tree in Cadzow Forest. The form of the signature indicates that it was added after August 1838 when the Scottish Academy received its Royal warrant.

For notes on the location and other Cadzow pictures see entry for Cat No 12

1   According to plaque attached to frame

2   Undertaken by Claire Plumb 1987 (SUA and RSAMD archives). No mention of the picture was found in the Minute Books of the Glasgow Athenaeum

3   In the 1871-2 *Post Office Glasgow Directory* the Bedford Hotel is listed at 54 St George's Place

4   For more on its history see James Lauder *The Glasgow Athenaeum — A Sketch of Fifty Year's Work (1847-1897)* Glasgow   1897

5   Soon after the move the Athenaeum split into two organisations, the Royal Scottish Academy of Music and Drama, and the Glasgow and West of Scotland College of Commerce

6   If Fraser's claim that the commission occurred when James Lumsden was Lord Provost, the date would have to be *c*1843-6

18

CASTLE CAMPBELL   ?1838

oil on prepared board

23.5 × 30.8 (9¼ × 12⅛)

lent by Dundee Art Galleries and Museums

Prov: Gibson Bequest 1927   *(8/27)*

Exb: 1947 Dundee   (81)

It is likely that this oil sketch of Castle Campbell from the west was done during McCulloch's visit to Dollar in the early autumn of 1838. In a letter[1] to his friend Daniel Macnee, McCulloch explained that he and John (probably John C Brown the Glasgow landscape painter see p 18) '. . . were at Castle Campbell for ten days. I got a very fine subject and intended to have made a first rate sketch but the weather was so very bad that for some days I hardly got anything done the consequence was I lost the feeling I commenced with and am afraid made a very poor sketch that is having a want of work on it and I hope to make the picture something'.

He was presumably happy with the finished painting for one of his nine exhibits at the RSA the following February (1839) was (165) *Castle Campbell.* The present small oil may be the 'poor sketch' to which the artist refers in the letter quoted above, in which case the 1839 RSA exhibit (now untraced)[2] was of the same view. McCulloch returned at least one more time to the castle, in the autumn of 1853 (see Cat No 36).

When McCulloch first went to Castle Campbell it was already considered to be one of the most picturesque and romantic ruins in Britain. Formerly known as Castle Gloom, this fortress of the powerful Campbell clan is a basically 15th century structure built on a precipitous rock almost encircled by a deep natural ravine. In the 19th century rushing torrents and dense woods challenged the tourist in search of a pathway up to the castle and to the anticipated spectacular view of the surrounding countryside. Today, a modern approach road allows access by motor vehicle, and considerable repairs and rebuilding have changed the silhouette of the castle as recorded by McCulloch.

1   See p 18

2   It was one of the four McCulloch oils acquired from that year's RSA exhibition by APFAS. Purchased for £60, it was awarded in the prize draw to Alexander Goodsir, Secretary of the British Linen Co, Edinburgh (APFAS *Report* 1838-9)

19

AN ISLAND KEEP   1843

oil on canvas

71.1 × 91.8 (28 × $36\frac{1}{8}$)

signed and dated lower left (on piece of driftwood)
Horatio McCulloch RSA 1843

lent by Renfrew District Council

Prov[1]: Presented to Paisley Art Gallery by Paisley
branch of the British Legion through Lord
Glentanar 1949   *(A283)*

The composition is probably imaginary although
perhaps based on a real castle in the West of Scotland.
Gylen near Oban and Dunollie in Oban Bay have both
been suggested. Whilst the influence of Rev Thomson
(see p 11) is evident in the heavy impasto of the sea
and rock, the thinner application of paint in the
background hills and stormy sky is individual to
McCulloch.

1   Part of a printed label attached to the stretcher seems to
relate to a bequest 'OF THE SETTLE . . . ./[T]ERMS OF THE
WIL[L]/[GEOR]GE,
FIRST BARON . . . ./BY THE TRUSTEES/[T]HE TERMS OF
TH[E] . . . ./and in ink *[McCu]lloch RSA
1843* and (?) *Glentanar'*

20

CADZOW FOREST   *c*1843

oil on canvas[1]

42 × 62.3 ($16\frac{1}{2}$ × $24\frac{1}{2}$)

signed lower right *H M?Culloch.*

lent from a private collection

Prov: Acquired at auction, probably in Montrose, *c* 1950; inherited by present owners

A contemporary description of McCulloch's 1843 RSA exhibit (437) *Scene in Cadzow Forest − Evening*[2] suggests a similar composition if not this actual picture: 'The exquisitely graduated vista opening through the glorious old trees on a deep golden sky − the distribution of colour so fine and so harmonious − the forcible painting of the trees in the left foreground − the rendering of the damp decay consuming the hollow trunk − the rent off branch − the water plants resting their broad leaves on the surface of the pool − if all these things be not instinct with nature we know not what nature is . . .'

Later in 1843 one of McCulloch's Royal Academy exhibits was (289) *Scene in Cadrew* [sic] *Forest* and one of his Glasgow exhibits that year was similarly titled as was one of his Dublin exhibits.

For notes on Cadzow Forest and other Cadzow pictures by McCulloch see entry for Cat No 12

1 For technical report see p 103

2 Purchased by APFAS for £60 and received as a prize by William Muir, Merchant, Leith (APFAS *Report* 1843-4); 1867 Edinburgh Clark Exh (12) *Glade in Cadzow Forest* lent by William Muir Esq

21

LANDSCAPE *c*1845

oil on canvas

32 × 51.2 ($11\frac{7}{8}$ × $20\frac{1}{8}$)

lent by Allan Caddy

Prov: With C Ward, Friargate, Derby *c*1976 from
whom purchased by present owner

THE CLYDE AT ERSKINE FERRY *c*1845

oil on panel

32.4 × 45.8 ($12\frac{5}{8}$ × 18)

signed lower left centre *H M*ᶜ*Culloch*

lent by Glasgow Art Gallery and Museum

22

Prov: Possibly a picture sold 1 Feb 1850 to 'David
Thompson Esq Glasgow a small picture Ferry
on the Clyde £7' (Account Book); John H
Downes probably by 1882 (see *Exh*); presented
by him Dec 1892   *Reg No 690*

Exh: (?)1882 Glasgow GIFA *19 Erskine Ferry* [Lent
by J H Downes][1]; 1894 Glasgow GIFA (592)
The Clyde near Erskine Ferry

1 No owner named in the catalogue, but No 18 in the same
exhibition was *In Skye* the title of another picture by
McCulloch owned by J H Downes and exhibited again in
Glasgow in 1911 (176)

23

PERTH FROM THE SOUTH   *c1845*

oil over pencil on canvas

37.1 × 58.4 (14⅝ × 23)

lent by Perth Museum and Art Gallery

Prov: (?)P R Drummond by 1867 (see ***Exh***);
presented by Mr Herbert Pullar, Dunbarney
1939   *(1/132)*

Exh: (?)1867 Edinburgh Clark Exh (66) *View of
Perth,* lent by P R Drummond Esq

A view of Perth after McCulloch was published as a colour lithograph by P R Drummond in 1869 (see illus). The lithograph is so like the present painting that it seems certain that this is the oil owned by Drummond[1].

The view from Moncrieff Hill was a standard one for book illustrations. McCulloch would have been familiar with Thomas Allom's view (see illus) in Beattie's *Scotland* (London 1838), and with the engraving after D O Hill (see illus) in Sir Thomas Dick Lauder's *The Royal Progress in Scotland* (Edinburgh 1843). McCulloch's viewpoint is almost identical to that selected by Hill and all three artists depict harvesters in the foreground.

McCulloch has taken great care with the drawing of the architectural and natural features of the scene. This allows a dating of between *c*1842 and 1848[2]. The prison building featured to the left is depicted as it appeared after an extension was added in 1841-2. Immediately below the prison, ships are clearly evident in the tidal basin (the site of the present-day Perth harbour), work on which started *c*1840 and was completed by 1845. By 1848, at least three rail routes entered Perth within the scope of McCulloch's view, but these are not depicted.

Engraving after D O Hill
1843

P R Drummond lithograph after McCulloch 1869

Engraving after T Allom 1838

Before the above topographical information was received, a date of *c*1845 had seemed probable, both for stylistic reasons and because in the 1840s McCulloch appears to have been planning to produce a series of town prospects for engraving. However only one plate is known to have been issued, a view of Kelso published in 1849 (Cat No 32). Other townscapes done around this date include the 1845 Edinburgh street scenes (Cat Nos 24-6) and a view of Edinburgh from Corstorphine Hill (Exh 1840 RSA 83).

1   In the McCulloch sale 7 Dec 1867 lot 88 was *View of Perth from Moncrieff Hill* bt Smith £15.15s (now untraced) which was presumably another version of this painting

2   The topographical information for this entry was kindly supplied by Robin Rodger

24

EDINBURGH CASTLE FROM THE GRASSMARKET
1845

pencil and watercolour heightened with white
bodycolour on wove paper
(several pieces pasted on one sheet)

41.1 × 36.9 (16¼ × 14½)

signed and dated lower centre (in pencil)
H MCulloch/August 16th 1845 inscribed lower left
(in ink) *To WF Watson Esq from Horatio MCulloch*
lower right *Unfinished* and (in pencil) *On the spot*

lent by The National Galleries of Scotland

Prov: W F Watson Bequest 1886   *(D2650)*

Ref: Watson *Catalogue* 1865 p 2 (159)

In this drawing of Edinburgh Castle, McCulloch has
overcome the difficulty he had with architectural
perspective in his Glasgow Cathedral view done some
fifteen years earlier (Cat No 1). That he chose to draw
the castle from the same spot selected by David
Roberts in 1828[1] probably has no significance, for this
was a standard view and was depicted by numerous
artists from the 18th century onwards. However the use
of white bodycolour, and the limited range and sparing
application of colour may derive from Roberts.

After he moved to Edinburgh in 1838, McCulloch
painted several distant views of the city, but this
drawing and the others owned by W F Watson (eg Cat
Nos 25, 26) are his only known Edinburgh street
scenes and were presumably done at Watson's request.

1 Guiterman and Llewellyn *David Roberts* London 1986 (24)
   repr pl 12 (colour)

THE WHITE HORSE CLOSE, EDINBURGH   1845

pencil and watercolour heightened with white bodycolour on greenish-grey wove paper

25.8 × 35.5 (10¼ × 14)

signed and inscribed lower left (in ink) *To W F Watson Esq from H. McCulloch* lower right *unfinished sketch* and (in pencil) *on the spot 1845*

lent by The National Galleries of Scotland

Prov: W F Watson Bequest 1886   *(D2652)*

Exb: 1981 Edinburgh NGS *Drawings from the Bequest of W F Watson* (20)

Ref: Watson *Catalogue* 1865 p 24 (148)

The 17th century White Horse Close, Canongate, now much restored, was clearly becoming dilapidated when McCulloch made this sketch.

25

THE COWGATE EDINBURGH, WITH EPISCOPAL CHAPEL   *c*1845

pencil and watercolour heightened with white bodycolour on greenish-grey wove paper

28.9 × 20.4 (11⅜ × 8)

signed lower centre (in ink) *H McCulloch* inscribed along right edge (in ink in another hand) *Original signed sketch of Cowgate Edinburgh/with Episcopal Chapel by Horatio McCulloch RSA*

lent by The National Galleries of Scotland

Prov: WF Watson Bequest 1886   *(D2290)*

Ref: ? Watson *Catalogue* 1865 p 24 (152) as 'sketch in sepia'

The church is St Patrick's, Cowgate

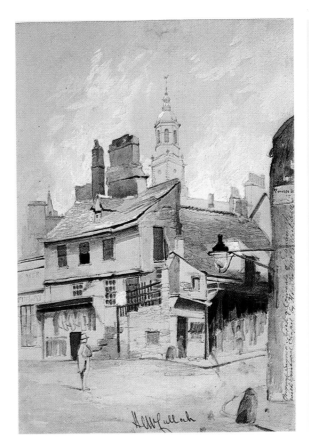

26

27

THE SCENE OF THE DOUGLAS TRAGEDY   *c*1845

pen and brown wash on off-white wove paper

16.8 × 24.7 (6⅝ × 9⅝)

signed lower centre (in ink) *HMC* inscribed lower left (in ink) *Douglas Tragedy the Scene* and lower right *Unfinished Sketch*

lent by The National Galleries of Scotland

Prov: WF Watson Bequest 1886   *(D2391)*

Ref: James Morrison 'Horatio McCulloch — Painter of the Highland Landscape' *Seer* June 1980 repr p 16

The inscribed title possibly refers to a play by John Home *Douglas: a tragedy,* first performed in Edinburgh in 1756.

28

LOCH LOMOND   1846

oil on canvas

27.2 × 56 (10¾ × 22)

signed and dated lower right *H McCulloch Sept 9 1846*

lent by the Hunterian Art Gallery, University of Glasgow

Prov: (?) Presented by J A McCallum *c*1948, certainly acquired by 1950   *(80.120 34/8)*

Ref: Donnelly p 6, pl 9

Previously called *Loch Etive and Ben Cruachan,* the view is correctly identified as Loch Lomond from the south. For notes on the location and other Loch Lomond subjects by McCulloch, see entry for Cat No 47.

This picture was painted *en route* to the Black Mount Deer Forest and Rannoch Moor, where the artist made another study from nature (Cat No 29). These studies show McCulloch's immediate response to the scene before him and to the unsettled weather he was experiencing on his trip.

29

THE ENTRANCE TO GLENCOE FROM RANNOCH MOOR 1846

oil on canvas[1]

34.6 × 60.6 ($13\frac{5}{8}$ × $23\frac{7}{8}$)

signed and dated lower left *H McCulloch Sept. 16 1846*

lent from a private collection

Prov: (?) Acquired in the mid 19th century by either John Gordon or Emily Gordon, Lady Cathcart[2]; by descent to present owners

Ref: Irwin pl 178; Donnelly p 6

The title suggested by the Irwins *Rannoch Moor, Glen Etive and the Meall A Bhuiridh Massif* is correct. The distant white building in the centre of the picture is the Kingshouse Hotel (5 miles from the entrance to Glencoe) beyond which is Glen Etive on the left of the picture behind the small building (Blackrock Cottage) on the brow of the hill[3].

Painted on 16 September 1846, a week after a Loch Lomond picture (Cat No 28), this must have been one of several studies made in the Glencoe region that autumn which were to be the basis for McCulloch's exhibits in Edinburgh the following spring (eg Cat No 30).

1 For technical report see p 103

2 The framemaker's label of Aitken Dott 14 & 16 South St David Street dates the frame to after 1863 (when the Edinburgh firm's premises at No 16 South St David Street were extended to include No 14). Another McCulloch oil in the same collection as this one has the same framemaker's label, perhaps suggesting that the two were acquired from Aitken Dott after 1863, (McCulloch's Account Book records many sales to Aitken Dott in the 1850s and 60s, often noted as 'a small picture'), or simply that the present picture was reframed sometime after 1863.

3 Location identified by Tarn Brown 1987

30

MISTY CORRIES — HAUNTS OF THE RED DEER
1847

oil on canvas

138.8 × 195.8 (54$\frac{5}{8}$ × 77$\frac{1}{8}$)

signed and dated lower right *H McCulloch 1847*
(last number indistinct)

*lent by the Shipley Art Gallery, Gateshead (Tyne
and Wear Museums Service)*

Prov: Purchased from the artist by Alexander Hill
(see *Exb*); presented to the Shipley Art Gallery
20 July 1933 by George Henderson   *(F9367)*

Exb: 1847 Edinburgh RSA (230) *Misty Corries —
Haunts of the Red Deer Sold to Mr Alexander
Hill . . . ;* 1848 London[1] FE (312) *Misty Corries —
Haunts of the Red Deer* H McCulloch £200

Ref: *Scotsman* 6 March 1847; Fraser pp 27 and 30

This highly romantic rendering of mountain scenery
provoked a rapturous review in the *Scotsman*. The
writer begins 'Here is the very poetry of the pencil' and
proceeds to describe the virtues of the painting
concluding 'High and vigorous is the thought of the
entire subject, and it is embodied in one of the noblest
specimens of broad and massy handling that ever hung
on the walls of the Academy'.

The painting is now sadly disfigured because of the
artist's extensive use of bitumen (see technical report
p 103) and by the unsuccessful attempts of picture
restorers to remedy this and other technical defects.

The composition probably derives from the artist's
1846 sketching trip to Rannoch Moor, Glencoe and the
Black Mount Deer Forest (see Cat No 29).

1   A handwritten label on stretcher reads 'Misty Corries —
Haunts of the Red Deer/By MacCulloch/Exhibited at the
Free Institution in London/in 1848 [W Olde?] Sept 1 1848'.
Presumably sent to the exhibition by Alexander Hill

SCENE IN THE HIGHLANDS 1848

watercolour and bodycolour on pale grey paper
pasted on card

13.4 × 24.1 (5½ × 9½)

signed and dated lower left *1848 H MC* [?] *June
30th* (indistinct)

lent from a private collection

Prov: 'Found in the attic' by present owner

LANDSCAPE 1848 oil

An oil painting dated 1848[1] (see illus) derives from this
watercolour. In the oil McCulloch has made changes to
the outline of the hills, moved the castle to a more
prominent position and introduced a figure group, a
boat and other decorative details, but the basic design
is the same.

The drawing was probably done on-the-spot and is
of an actual place — many of McCulloch's watercolours
are 'compositions' — but the location has not been
identified. The inscribed date is partly obscured by a
dash of white bodycolour, an indication that McCulloch
made later additions to the original drawing.

1 Christie's Scotland 11 Dec 1986 lot 51

32

William Forrest (1805-89) after Horatio McCulloch

THE TOWN OF KELSO   1849

line engraving

41 × 56.9 ($16\frac{1}{8}$ × $22\frac{7}{8}$)

engraved inscriptions lower left (margin)
H McCulloch R.S.A. lower centre *Kelso. Published
by J. Mackintosh Carver & Gilder, 1849* lower right
W Forrest and below this *To His Grace The Duke Of
Roxburobe* [sic] *This View of/THE TOWN OF KELSO/
Is by His Grace's Permission most respectfully
inscribed by the Publisher* and lower right *Printed
by A. McGlashon*[1]

lent by The National Galleries of Scotland

Prov: National Gallery of Scotland   *(RNP 492)*

Fraser tells us that McCulloch was in Kelso in 1850, staying with his friend Dr Mackenzie but this engraving indicates at least one previous visit.

The view which he selected was an obvious one. Turner had sketched Kelso from almost exactly the same spot for his 1832 watercolour, which McCulloch would have known from the engraving after it in Scott's *Poetical Works* (1833-4).

The view features Rennie's bridge (1800-3) over the Tweed, the town, the ancient Abbey and in the distance, between the trees on the left of the picture, Floors Castle, the seat of the Duke of Roxburgh, to whom the plate is dedicated.

The circumstances leading to the publication of this plate are not known. The existence of other town prospects in oil by McCulloch (eg Cat No 23) might mean that he was hoping to provide material for a series of engravings, or this one may simply have been an isolated commission from the publisher.

McCulloch's original design for the engraving, probably an oil painting, has not been traced and is not recorded in contemporary sources. Other townscapes done around this date include the 1845 Edinburgh street scenes (Cat Nos 24-6) and a view of Edinburgh from Corstorphine Hill, Exh 1840 RSA (83).

1   Probably Alexander McGlashon, steel and copperplate
     printer, who settled in Edinburgh *c*1838 and was employed
     by APFAS to print the engraving after McCulloch's *Loch-an-
     Eilin* (illus p 17) in 1838-9 (APFAS *Report* 1839-40)

33

LOWLAND RIVER — SUNSET   1851

oil on canvas

99 × 149.9 (39 × 59)

signed and dated lower left *H McCulloch. 1851*

lent by The National Galleries of Scotland

Prov: Purchased from the artist 28 Feb 1851 by Robert Cox £150[1]; his Bequest 1872 · *(587)*

Exh: 1851 Edinburgh RSA (91) *Lowland River — Sunset;* 1852 Glasgow WSA (193) *Lowland River, Autumn Evening, Sunset* the property of Robert Cox Esq WS, Edinburgh; 1867 Edinburgh Clark Exh (18) *A Lowland River — Sunset* lent by Robert Cox Esq; 1868 Glasgow GIFA (21) *The Lowland River* the property of Robert Cox Esq Edinburgh

Ref: *Scotsman* 8 March 1851; *Edinburgh Evening Courant* 8 March 1851; *Glasgow Sentinel* 8 Feb 1868; *Glasgow Herald* 20 Feb 1868; Fraser pl 9 and text opposite

According to the Clark Exhibition Catalogue this imaginary scene was based on studies done on the Water of Leith in 1849, which were shown in Clark's 1867 exhibition (14), (32) and (72) and which were probably similar to the study (Cat No 35) done two years later.

The finished work was much admired when it was first exhibited — '. . . remarkable for its unity and breadth of effect, combined with the careful finish of the various parts' — and received equal praise in 1868 as characteristic of 'The summer pride of his genius'. This second appearance in a public exhibition coincided with the decision of RAPFAS to issue an engraving after *Lowland River* for subscribers (see Cat No 34).

1   Account Book

34

William Forrest (1805-89) after Horatio McCulloch

A LOWLAND RIVER

line engraving

plate size 54.6 × 69.8 (21¾ × 27½)
image size 38.1 × 57.8 (15 × 22¾)

engraved signature and date lower left (image)
H. McCulloch 1851; engraved inscription lower left
(margin) *PAINTED BY HORATIO MACCULLOCH
RSA* lower right (margin) *ENGRAVED BY WILLIAM
FORREST* lower centre (margin) *A Lowland River/
From a painting by Horatio McCulloch RSA in the
possession of Robert Cox Esq./Engraved exclusively
for the members of the Royal Association for
Promotion of the Fine Arts in Scotland for the year
1869-70*

lent by Glasgow Art Gallery and Museum

Prov: Acquired by 1901, no record of provenance *(a-
       2a)*

Ref: RAPFAS *Report* 1868-9

For notes on *A Lowland River* see previous entry.

35

STUDY ON THE WATER OF LEITH   1853

oil on canvas

41 × 61.4 (16⅛ × 24⅛)

signed and dated lower left *H McCulloch.
August 9th 1853*

lent from a private collection

Prov: Possibly the picture 'Study on the Water of Leith
       at Bonnington' which was purchased from the
       artist by Mr Smith Register Street March 1854
       £20[1]; received as a gift by the present owners in
       1958

Although it is difficult to identify the exact spot today,
there is little doubt that the subject is the Water of
Leith, Edinburgh. Factory buildings and new houses
have been constructed since the mid 19th century, but
the character of the river and its banks is comparatively
unchanged. Willows and butterburs, so minutely
observed by McCulloch, are still to be found and the
water is just as tranquil.

A comparison between this 1853 study (and Cat No
36) and the two 1846 on-the-spot oil sketches (Cat Nos
28 and 29) shows how much the artist's method and
intention has changed. In the 1846 paintings a
momentary effect of the weather is expressed in rapid
brushwork, the pictures themselves apparently
(although not actually) dashed off in a moment. In the
Water of Leith and *Castle Campbell* measured thought
and carefully observed detail produce the opposite
effect, one of timelessness.

1 Account Book. However a printed framemaker's label on
    the stretcher which reads 'James Walker, Edinburgh,
    Assembly Rooms, George St.' may indicate that James
    Walker was the buyer (although he seems to have ceased
    in business in about 1842 — see Index to FRAMEMAKERS
    p 106)

36

CASTLE CAMPBELL 1853

oil on canvas

53.3 × 45.5 (21 × 17⅞)

signed and dated lower right *H. McCulloch./Sept.* 7.
1853

lent by Professor A J M Sykes

Prov: Purchased at auction from Edmiston's Glasgow[1]
by the present owner

For an earlier Castle Campbell subject and for notes on
the location see Cat No 18. In the present painting the
artist has chosen a lower viewpoint, slightly further to
the south-west of the castle, which enabled him to
indulge his passion for trees.

The painting is not recorded in the artist's Account
Book unless it was one of 'two small pictures painted
from nature at Dollar' which were purchased by Robert
Cox 13 Jan 1854 for £40.

1 Sale record not traced but on the back of the canvas is
written 'lot 133' in white chalk

37

DRUMLANRIG CASTLE DUMFRIESSHIRE *c*1855

oil on prepared board[1]

40.6 × 61 (16 × 24)

lent by the Duke of Buccleuch and Queensberry KT

Prov: (?)McCulloch sale 7 Dec 1867 lot 93
*Drumlanrig Castle Dumfriesshire finished study
from nature* bt Churnside £24 13s 6d[2];
bequeathed by Major General Granville Egerton
to Margaret Buccleuch 1951[3]

Exh: (?)1867 Edinburgh Clark Exh (62) *Drumlanrig
Castle, painted on the spot* − Mr McCulloch's
Estate

Looking north over the Nith Valley this view shows the
south front of the castle, which was built over an earlier
stronghold in the late 17th century by William Douglas,
1st Duke of Queensberry. Although neither signed nor
documented this painting can be confidently attributed
to McCulloch on stylistic grounds and dated to the
1850s. McCulloch also painted nearby Morton Castle[4],
another property belonging to the Duke of Buccleuch.
Both paintings were in the artist's possession when he
died.

Several watercolour views of Drumlanrig done by
McCulloch's friend William Leighton Leitch some ten
years earlier are in the Drumlanrig Castle collection.

1   Printed label 'Winsor & Newton, 38 Rathbone Place'

2   Annotated Sale Cat, V & A Library (23D)

3   Note pasted to back of picture in handwriting of Margaret,
widow of John 7th Duke of Buccleuch (information kindly
supplied by His Grace the Duke of Buccleuch and
Queensberry)

4   McCulloch sale 7 Dec 1867 lot 78 bt Bonnar
£16 16s; now untraced

38

KNOCK CASTLE AND THE SOUND OF SLEAT 1854

pencil, watercolour and bodycolour on buff paper

35 × 50.5 (13¾ × 19⅞) (sight)

signed and dated lower left *H. McCulloch Sept 30th. 1854*

lent by Dundee Art Galleries and Museums (Orchar Collection)

Prov: J G Orchar probably by 1867[1] (see *Exh*); his Bequest to the burgh of Broughty Ferry 1896 *(177)*

Exh: (?) 1867 Edinburgh Clark Exh (85) as *Dunskiach Isle of Skye 1854* (watercolour) lent by J G Orchar

Ref: Fraser, text opposite pl 7; James Morrison 'Horatio McCulloch − Painter of the Highland Landscape' *Seer* June 1980 repr p 13

This is the study for an oil painting which was exhibited in Edinburgh the following spring[2]. The oil follows the watercolour quite closely in composition apart from the addition of fishing boats in the foreground.

In the drawing the buff tone of the paper is used as a positive element in the colour composition, onto which the artist has sparingly applied a range of browns, yellows and greens in contrast to the rich blue in the distance. The broad brush-strokes in the foreground and more detailed work over the pencil

Photograph in Fraser (pl 7)

outlines in the middle and far distance create a strong feeling of recession.

The medieval Knock Castle, a residence of the MacDonalds of Sleat, Isle of Skye, was already a picturesque ruin when McCulloch drew this view looking across Knock Bay towards the castle, the Sound of Sleat and the hills of Knoydart in the distance.

1   Its sale is not recorded in McCulloch's Account Book

2   RSA 1855 (13) (incorrectly identified by Rinder and McKay as this picture). It was sold to George Baird 23 June 1855 £150 (Account Book); mentioned in *The Art Journal* 1855 p 154 and repr Fraser pl 7 (see illus). Present whereabouts unknown

39

DUNSTAFFNAGE CASTLE   1854

oil on canvas[1]

66.3 × 121.2 (26⅛ × 47¾)

signed and dated lower left *H McCulloch 1854*

lent by Glasgow Art Gallery and Museum

Prov: Commissioned by David Hutcheson and
completed by Jan 1855[2]; David Adam Smith;
inherited by his sister Mrs Janet Rodger; her
Bequest 1901   *Reg No 997*

Exh: 1855 Edinburgh RSA (158) *Dunstaffnage Castle
Argyleshire* the property of D Hutcheson Esq
Glasgow

Ref: *Edinburgh Evening Courant* 13 March 1855;
Scotsman 14 March 1855; Fraser pl 3 and text
opposite

The medieval castle of Dunstaffnage, 3 miles north of
Oban, was an obvious choice of subject for the
painting's first owner, the Glasgow entrepreneur David
Hutcheson. His highly successful steamship company
had created a busy tourist centre out of the small
fishing village of Oban. Hutcheson expressed his
fondness for Oban and district in verse and was
eventually buried there. According to Fraser (*loc cit*) 'It
was during a walk one summer evening (1854) along
the shore of Loch Etive with Macculloch, that
Mr Hutcheson commissioned him to paint this picture.

Macculloch spent two days in making a careful study in
water-colour of the castle and surrounding scenery on
the spot[3]. The picture was painted the following winter,
and formed one of the most attractive features of the
exhibition of the following spring, as it now does of
Mr Hutcheson's dining room.'

The view which Hutcheson and McCulloch admired
can still be seen although a modern housing estate
occupies the immediate foreground. The castle is
relatively unchanged and this view of it from the south-
west, showing the 13th century curtain wall, is much as
it would have looked when it was first built by the
Lords of Lorn in the mid 13th century. The colourful
history of the castle from its capture by Robert Bruce in
1309 to the imprisonment of Flora MacDonald there in
1746 earned Dunstaffnage a stanza in Scott's 'Lord of
the Isles' and ensured it a permanent place in the
tourist guide-books.

At least one previous visit to Dunstaffnage by
McCulloch seems likely. One of his 1847 Glasgow
exhibits was (192) *Highland Landscape, Dunstaffnage
Castle* the property of James Walker Esq, Edinburgh.

1 For technical report see p 103

2 Account Book 16 Jan 1855 'from David Hutcheson
Steamboat Proprietor, Glasgow for a picture of
Dunstaffnage Castle £60.' Framemaker's label of Aitken
Dott, 16 South St David Street

3 Presumably the watercolour included in the 1867
Edinburgh Clark Exh (89) *Dunstaffnage Castle, painted
on the spot* lent by Chas Hutchins Esq (now untraced)

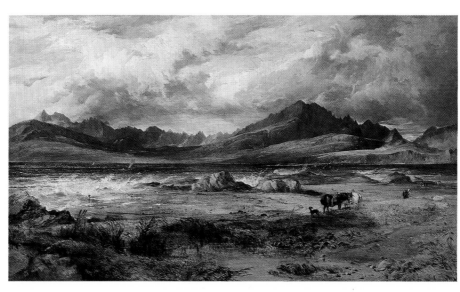

40

THE CUILLINS FROM ORD   ?1854

oil on canvas

71.1 × 121.9 (28 × 48)

signed lower left *H. McCulloch.*

lent by Glasgow Art Gallery and Museum

Prov: A G Macdonald (?) by 1867 (see *Exh*); his Bequest 1903   *Reg No 1052*

Exh: Possibly RSA 1854 (238) *The Coolin Mountains Isle of Skye*[1] bt by the Glasgow Art Union[2]; (?)1867 Edinburgh Clark Exh (11) *A Breezy Day in Skye* lent by A G Macdonald Esq; 1897 London Earls Court *Victorian Era Exhibition* (72) *Loch Slapin and Coolin Mountains* lent by A G Macdonald

McCulloch's first recorded painting of Skye was *Cullin Hills from Gillian Bay Isle of Skye* which he sold to William Dennistoun on 28 January 1848 for £60[3]. This sale is the first entry in the artist's Account Book and coincides with his marriage to Marcella McLellan of Gillian (the location depicted) and with the date of a commissioned work *View of the Coast of Sleat* (see illus p 21) which was lithographed for *Scotland Delineated*[4].

All these events suggest a first visit to Skye in 1847 (see p 22) after which year Skye titles occur regularly amongst McCulloch's works. This painting may be his 1854 RSA exhibit (238) of which the *Scotsman* critic wrote '. . . another excellent work, serrated hills are most skilfully treated, sky a perfect masterpiece of power and execution'[5]. Other recorded titles can be eliminated, because of the location (eg . . . from Gillian Bay, . . . from Dalavil) or because a contemporary description precludes the possibility of their being the present work.

When it entered the Gallery's collection the painting was titled *Loch Slapin and Coolin Mountains* but it is correctly identified as the Cuillins from Ord, on the north coast of Sleat. The water is Loch Eishort and the view is taken from the beach at Ord very near the house owned by Charles Macdonald, Marcella McCulloch's uncle, His daughter Flora married McCulloch's friend, the poet Alexander Smith, in 1857. Of the famous mountain range Smith wrote '. . . the entire range of the Cuchullins — the outline wild, splintered, jagged, as if drawn by a hand shaken by terror or frenzy'[6]; McCulloch has depicted them accurately whilst slightly exaggerating the jagged nature of the peaks.

1 Usually written as Cuillin today, the many spelling variations include Coolin, Cullin, Culinn and Cuchullin

2 Account Book July 1854 '. . . from Mr Kidston Glasgow for Ballence of picture sold to Glasgow Art Union "Coolin Hills Skye" £100' (the total amount paid is not recorded in the Account Book)

3 Account Book. The picture, now untraced, was exhibited RSA 1848 (298) and WSA 1848 (90)

4 See p 22. The painting (untraced) was exhibited WSA 1848 (155) and sold to William Wilson of Bankknock Nov 1848 (Account Book). The view is characteristic of the north coast of Sleat but the exact location has not been identified

5 *Scotsman* 18 Feb 1854

6 *A Summer in Skye* London 1865, vol 1 p 132

41

STORM ON A HIGHLAND COAST, ISLE OF SKYE 1855

oil on canvas

87.6 × 134.6 (34½ × 53)

signed and dated lower right *H. McCulloch. 1855*

lent from a private collection

Prov: (?)Bt by the Glasgow Art Union 1856 £200[1]; Sotheby's Gleneagles 31 Aug 1973 lot 246 bt Patrick Bourne and acquired from him by the present owners

Exh: (?)1856 Edinburgh RSA (59) *Storm on a Highland Coast, Isle of Skye*; 1856 London *Storm on a Highland Coast − Ben Blavon* [sic] *Isle of Skye*[2]

Ref: (?)*The Art Journal* 1856 p 180 (quoted below) and p 280; *Scotsman* 8 March 1856; *Edinburgh Evening Courant* 18 March 1856

Reviewing the RSA exhibition, *The Art Journal* critic chose McCulloch's work to illustrate his remark 'In many of the landscapes we find a degree of force and originality . . . one of the first of this class that struck us was No.59, Storm on a Highland Coast . . . a large picture the subject being a passage of wild scenery under the effect of a storm in which the drifting of the rain is forcibly described'.

The subject is a closer view of Ben Blaven than that depicted in Cat No 40. Whilst the latter is an accurate delineation of the scenery (despite alterations to the foreground), in this painting, faithful recording of topography is subordinated to the portrayal of tempestuous weather on a desolate shore. McCulloch has achieved this through contrasting heavy impasto and thinly applied glazes, deep blues and pale ochres, and through skilful brushwork, both broadly painted and finely detailed. It is one of the artist's most successful expressions of the sublime in Scottish landscape.

1 Account Book as *Blaven Isle of Skye* − several small payments were made from March 1856, the balance paid on 3 Dec 1856

2 *The Art Journal* 1856 p 280, review of Glasgow Art Union prize pictures on exhibition at OWCS

Photograph 1860s

LOCHALINE CASTLE   1856

oil on canvas

53.3 × 76.2 (21 × 30)

signed and dated lower right *H. McCulloch. 1856* (last number indistinct)

lent by Glasgow Art Gallery and Museum

Prov: (?)Purchased from the artist May 1857 by RAPFAS £70[1]; the late Miss N W Tannahill sale Morrison McChlery & Co Glasgow 18 March 1960 lot 124 as *A Highland Glen with burn and ruined castle* purchased £18   *Reg No 3122*

Exh: (?)1857 Edinburgh RSA (114) *Loch Aline Castle, Sound of Mull*; 1974 Knox Exh (36); 1977 Bordeaux, Musée de Beaux Arts *Le Peinture Britannique de Gainsborough à Bacon* (117) repr

Ref: (?)*Edinburgh Evening Courant* 10 March 1857

Although the date on the painting is difficult to decipher it is probable that this was McCulloch's 1857 exhibit, the description of which in the *Edinburgh Evening Courant* reads: '. . . the brawling stream foaming along its rocky bed, the old weather-beaten tower crowning the steep bank, and the beautiful wooded valley receding for miles till lost in the indistinctness of distance . . .'.

Several small pictures of the subject are recorded and McCulloch appears to have been working on another large version in the year of his death: in the Clark exhibition Edinburgh, 1867, No 60 was '*Loch Aline Castle* lent by Mr M'Culloch's Estate' and captioned 'Intended for the Exhibition of the RS Academy the present year'.

Kinlochaline Castle, Morven, stands at the head of Loch Aline, a small sea loch off the Sound of Mull. McCulloch's view is considerably altered today. The castle keep was restored in 1890, trees have grown up on both sides of the River Aline and a bridge has been constructed to take the road which leads along the lochside to Ardtornish House and castle. Photographs taken in the 1860s[2] however show the castle in an even more ruinous state than it appears in this picture (see illus).

1   Account Book 28 May 1857 'Lochalin Castle Sound of Mull £70'. In March 1857 he sold 'a small picture of Lochalin Castle' to Aitken Dott, the Edinburgh framemaker, for £17 (Account Book) which was probably the study for the present work

2   In the Gertrude Smith Album (National Monuments Record of Scotland)

43

GLEN AFFRIC   1857

oil on canvas[1]

84.2 × 122 ($33\frac{1}{8}$ × 48)

signed and dated lower left *H McCulloch. 1857*

lent by Glasgow Art Gallery and Museum

Prov: Presented by Miss Russell 1927   *Reg No 1713*

It has not been possible to identify this painting with any of McCulloch's exhibited titles nor with the pictures listed in his Account Book. Whilst the signature appears to be genuine, the attribution should be considered provisional until better-documented comparative works are located.

1   For technical report see p 103

44

THE CLYDE FROM DALNOTTAR HILL   1858

oil on canvas

111.5 × 182.5 ($43\frac{7}{8}$ × $71\frac{7}{8}$)

lent by the Clydesdale Bank PLC

Prov: Commissioned in 1857 by James Tennant Caird
and paid for 15 May 1858 £420[1]; (?)T Graham
Young by 1888 (see *Exh*): G H T Macleod by
1958 (see *Exh*); with Ian MacNicol by Oct 1959
from whom acquired by present owners

Exh: 1859 Edinburgh RSA (162) *The Clyde from
Dalnotter* [sic] *Hill* the property of James
Tennant Caird Esq of Greenock; (?)1888
Glasgow *International Exhibition* (211) lent by
T Graham Young; 1958 Helensburgh (and tour)
The Artist and the River Clyde (23) lent by G H
T Macleod[2]; 1972 Glasgow Art Gallery *Scenic
Aspects of the River Clyde* (47) lent by the
Clydesdale Bank

Ref: *Edinburgh Evening Courant* 26 Feb 1859;
Scotsman 1 March 1859; Fraser pp 22 and 29

For notes on the subject and other versions of this
view, see the entry for Cat No 3.

A commission from the Greenock shipbuilder, James
Tennant Caird, allowed McCulloch to paint this
favourite scene apparently for the first time since his
departure from Glasgow more than twenty years

previously. Whilst the handsome price paid by his new
patron must have contributed to the exuberant tone of
McCulloch's letter of thanks, his delight at being asked
for this particular view sounds sincere: 'I might say a
great deal on the subject of the obligation I owe you
for giving me an opportunity of painting a scene I had
long dreamed of but will content myself with saying I
truly thank you . . .' It is clear from the letter and from
the attached receipt[3] that Caird had placed an advance
order for the picture, perhaps choosing from one or
other of the 'two studies of the Clyde from
Old Kilpatrick' which McCulloch sold to Mr Aidie the
Edinburgh picture dealer[4] in November 1857.
Cat No 45 may be one of them; the second is untraced.

The 1859 RSA catalogue states that this painting was
to be engraved by William Forrest, but no such
engraving is known to have been produced.

1   Account Book '. . . From J Caird Esq. Greenock for a
Picture of the Clyde from Old Kilpatrick £420.'

2   Recorded as signed *H. McCulloch* (and either a date or
RSA) in Exh Cat. Although a signature is noted in the 1972
Glasgow Exh Cat, its compiler may have taken the
information from the 1958 Cat

3   Letter and receipt both dated 15 May 1858 together with
undated and unattributed (?)Glasgow newspaper cuttings
dealing with the painting at length (SRA, Mitchell Library)

4   Account Book 25 Nov 1857 '. . . from Mr Aidie Hanover
Street for two studies of the Clyde from Old Kilpatrick
£37 10'

45

THE CLYDE FROM DALNOTTAR HILL   1857

oil over pencil on canvas

37.5 × 75.6 (14¾ × 29¾)

signed and dated lower right *H McCulloch. Sept.*
1857

lent from a private collection

Prov: Possibly one of 'two studies of the Clyde from
Old Kilpatrick' sold to Mr Aidie, Hanover St
Edinburgh 25 Nov 1857 £37 10s[1]; Sir James
Young (1811-83); by descent to his
granddaughter Helen Robertson (née Young);
inherited from her in 1987 by present owner

A study for Cat No 44. See that entry for further
information (the possibility that this was the picture
exhibited in the 1888 Glasgow exhibition rather than
Cat No 44 should not be ruled out).

1   Account Book

46

MY HEART'S IN THE HIGHLANDS   1860

oil on canvas

61 × 91.4 (24 × 36)

signed and dated lower left *H. M.Culloch 1860*

lent by Glasgow Art Gallery and Museum

Prov: Commissioned by RAPFAS[1] and paid for
5 Dec 1860 £100[2]; David Hutcheson by 1867
(see *Exb*); David Adam Smith; inherited by his
sister Mrs Janet Rodger; her Bequest 1901
Reg No 1001

Exb: 1867 Glasgow GIFA (173) *My Heart's in the
Highlands* the property of David Hutchison Esq;
1867 Edinburgh Clark Exh (56) *My Heart's in
the Highlands* lent by David Hutchison Esq;
1878 Glasgow GIFA (206) *My Heart's in the
Highlands* D Hutcheson; 1973-4 Stirling
MacRobert Art Centre *The Kailyard and the
Glue Pot* (19)

Ref: *Glasgow Herald* 5 and 16 Feb 1867; Fraser pl 8
and text opposite

The painting was engraved by William Forrest (see illus
p 112) for *Illustrated Songs of Robert Burns* (RAPFAS
1861 pl 3). A watercolour version in Paisley Art Gallery
(B40A) is probably a copy after the engraving.

According to Fraser, McCulloch had intended
originally to call this painting of an imaginary scene
'An Emigrant's Dream of his Highland Home'.

1   One of 'five pictures painted expressly for the society . . .
illustrative of 5 songs of Burns'
(*The Art Journal* 1 Sept 1861)

2   Account Book '. . . for a picture "My Heart's in the
Highlands" £100'

47

LOCH LOMOND   1861

oil on canvas

86.5 × 137.5 ($34\frac{1}{16}$ × $54\frac{1}{8}$)

signed and dated lower right *Horatio. McCulloch. 1861.*

lent by Glasgow Art Gallery and Museum

Prov: (?)The 'Loch Lomond' purchased by Michael Scott between July and Dec 1861 £300[1]; A G Macdonald by 1871; his Bequest 1903 *Reg No 1053*

Exh: 1871 Glasgow GIFA (25) *Loch Lomond from Boturich* lent by Baillie Macdonald; 1888 Glasgow *International Exhibition* (326) *Loch Lomond* lent by A G Macdonald; 1897 London Earls Court *Victorian Era Exhibition* (2) *Loch Lomond* lent by A G Macdonald; 1898 Glasgow *People's Palace Inaugural Art Exhibition* (49) lent by A G Macdonald; 1974 Knox Exh (35)

Ref: Roger Billcliffe *The Glasgow Boys* London 1985 p 27 pl 15

This view of Loch Lomond looks north-west over Inchmurrin Island and the many small wooded islands of the southern part of the loch towards Ben Lomond to the right in the picture and Ben Vorlich in the far distance. The artist positioned himself by the roadside below Mount Misery, about a mile north of Boturich just before Lorn Farm. The resulting on-the-spot study for this painting, which was done the previous year (Cat No 48), reveals the extent to which McCulloch has altered the topography in the finished work to create a more interesting composition. The study is an entirely faithful rendering of the scene, which has hardly altered during the intervening years. In it McCulloch records a fence leading down to the trees at the loch's shore. This fence is now a farm track but the steep slope of the field and the extent of the woodland here, and on the island of Inchmurrin, is very much the same today.

In the finished painting the artist has reshaped the foreground considerably, redistributed the trees, added large boulders, a little bridge and a cottage. The islands and mountains across the loch are fairly accurately rendered. A visually awkward patch of water in front of Ben Vorlich, quite prominent in the study, is toned down in the finished version. Likewise touches of pink in the sky and on the islands in the middle distance in the sketch are toned down in the finished work. Both paintings were X-rayed in 1987[2]. The results suggest that McCulloch made no significant changes in the course of painting either picture.

One of the best known of all Scottish beauty spots, Loch Lomond was a favourite sketching ground for McCulloch throughout his life. His earliest Loch Lomond exhibit was with the Glasgow Dilettanti Society in 1830[3] and after that Loch Lomond subjects appeared frequently amongst his exhibited works and amongst the private sales recorded in his Account Book[4]. When he first went there, around 1830, McCulloch would have taken a steam-boat from the Broomielaw in Glasgow, to Dumbarton, alighted there and transferred to a coach bound for Balloch. By 1860 he could catch one of the frequent trains from Glasgow direct to Balloch.

1   Account Book 1 July 1861 '. . . from Mr Scott Esq one hundred pounds to account of Picture of "Loch Lomond"; 31 July 1861 'Received from Michael Scott Esq as part payment of picture of "Lochlomond" £100'; 20 Dec 1861 '. . . From Michael Scott Esq as Payment in full of Picture of "Lochlomond" £100.'

2   By Tom Eddie and Dan Graham. See technical report p 103

3   See p 14 (and illus)

4   Sixteen or more Loch Lomond pictures can be listed from these sources alone, which makes identification of surviving examples a hazardous exercise

48

LOCH LOMOND   1860

oil on canvas

40.2 × 61 (16 × 24)

signed and dated lower left *Painted on the spot/H McCulloch 1860*

lent from a private collection

Prov: Purchased from the artist 22 July 1861 by Sir James Lumsden £42[1]; by descent to present owner

The study for Cat No 47; see that entry for a discussion of the subject. After many years as tenant, Sir James Lumsden acquired the Arden estate, Bonhill, on the western shore of Loch Lomond, in 1867. A 1915 inventory of Arden House includes this picture 'Horatio McCulloch, Original Oil Sketch. "Loch Lomond from Mount Misery" (valued at £150)[2].

1   Account Book 22 July 1861 'for a study "Loch Lomond" £42'

2   Lumsden Papers (GUA)

49

GLENCOE   1864

oil on canvas

112 × 183.3 (44 × 72)

signed and dated lower right *H. McCulloch 1864*
(indistinct)

lent by Glasgow Art Gallery and Museum

Prov: Sold to James Patrick Sept 1864 £420[1]; (his sale
?1869); David Adam Smith by 1875 (see *Exh*);
inherited by his sister Mrs Janet Rodger; her
Bequest 1901   *Reg No 1003*

Exh: 1865 Edinburgh RSA (425) *Glencoe* property of
James Patrick Esq of Kilmun; 1875 Glasgow
GIFA (275) lent by David A Smith Esq; 1908
Edinburgh *Scottish National Exh* (121); 1908
Newcastle; 1911 Rome *International Fine Art
Exhibition* (56) repr p 137 of souvenir; 1926
Edinburgh RSA *Centenary Exh* (132); 1926
Paisley Art Institute; 1935 Glasgow *Century of
Art* (19); 1939 London RA *Scottish Art* (177) repr
p 55 of souvenir; 1961 Glasgow Art Gallery
Scottish Painting (66); 1968/9 Ottawa National
Gallery *Three Centuries of Scottish Painting*
(30); 1976 Edinburgh RSA *150th Anniversary
Exhibition* (Academicians & Associates section,

6, repr); 1978 Edinburgh NGS *The Discovery of
Scotland* (9.19) repr cover and fig 106

Ref: *The Art Journal* 1865 pp 111-13; *Edinburgh
Evening Courant* 4 Feb 1865; *Scotsman* 15 Feb
1865; *Glasgow Sentinel* 20 Feb 1875; Fraser p 32
pl 18; McKay pp 269, 271 repr; Cursiter p 93
repr opp p 99; Charles Carter 'Monarch of Glen
and Gallery' *Country Life Annual* 1961 p 69 fig
1; William Gaunt *The Restless Century* London
1972 pl 124; Irwin pp 355-6 pl 179;
M Jacobs and M Warner *Art in Scotland* 1980;
Editor D Bindman *The Thames & Hudson
Encyclopaedia of Art* London 1985, repr

Of all McCulloch's landscapes *Glencoe* is the one which
has survived as a popular image. The picture has been
on public view almost without interruption since it
entered Glasgow's collection in 1901. It has been lent to
numerous exhibitions and has been repeatedly
reproduced, as book covers and illustrations, calendars,
cigarette cards, coloured prints and postcards.

A compelling representation of Scotland's most
famous glen, this view was already well known by the
1860s. Looking westwards from the rock platform
known as the Study, the mountains are the Three
Sisters of Glencoe and the road to the right in the

Lithograph in Lawson's *Scotland Delineated* 1847-54

picture is the old military road constructed in about 1750 when the massacre of Glencoe was still a remembered event.

When it was first exhibited in 1865 the critics were not happy with the colouring of *Glencoe* '. . . though perhaps a little tawny in colour throughout, is a noble Highland landscape' (*Scotsman*) and '. . . Glencoe is well composed but somewhat leathery in colouring' (*Edinburgh Evening Courant*). In reality the colouring is quite accurate for an autumn day in the Highlands. These criticisms perhaps indicate that McCulloch's avoidance of the brighter green pigments which had been on the market for some time[2] was beginning to make his work seem old fashioned.

Of this painting Fraser writes that it was done 'from studies made many years previously'. McCulloch's first recorded visit to Glencoe was a sketching trip made in the autumn of 1844 with his artist-friends John C Brown and William B Johnstone (see p 18). The following year both McCulloch and Brown exhibited Glencoe subjects, McCulloch first with the RSA (227) and later in the year with the WSA[3]. The lithograph after that *Glencoe* (see illus) shows that the mountains are seen from almost exactly the same point as in the present picture, but the arrangement of the foreground rocks is quite different, and in the later work a herd of deer replace the grazing sheep, perhaps an intentional comment on the actual replacement of sheep by deer in many Highland glens.

The artist revisited Glencoe in 1846 (see entry for Cat No 29) and a study made then was developed into a finished work, which was acquired (or had been commissioned) by David Hutcheson[4]. This may have been the picture sent to London for exhibition at the BI in 1848 (277) and which was noticed by the *Art Union* critic: 'The famous Glen is here brought forward

under the aspect of a dark and menacing sky, which communicates to the rocks and precipices a grandeur well beseeming their character. It is a picture somewhat peculiar in style, but original, and of unprecedented merit'. McCulloch exhibited one other Glencoe subject, in the early 1850s[5] and both this and the 1864 picture may have been based on the studies done in the 1840s.

1   Account Book 'Received from James Patrick Esq. of Benmore for a picture "Glencoe" £420.' Old label on back of frame (in ink) 'Glencoe the property of James Patrick Esq . . . [obscured by later label] . . .' Framemaker's label of Aitken Dott 14 & 16 South St David St, Edinburgh

2   See technical report p 103

3   (84) *Glencoe* the property of William Dennistoun; now untraced it was lithographed by R Carrick, in J P Lawson *Scotland Delineated* (London 1847-54)

4   Now untraced, its sale is not recorded in the Account Book (which commences Jan 1848) and it was therefore probably acquired in 1847. Exh 1862 Glasgow GIFA, 1863 Edinburgh RSA, 1867 Edinburgh Clark Exh (8) *Glencoe — Bridge of three waters 1847* David Hutcheson Esq (the study was No 13 in the Clark Exh and the lender given as Mr McCulloch's estate)

5   1852 Glasgow GIFA (284) *Glencoe, looking down, mist rising after rain* and 1853 Edinburgh RSA (155) *Glencoe looking down the Glen — Effect of mist rising after rain.* This was presumably the picture sold to Hill, MacLure and Macdonald in Sept 1852 for £50 (Account Book) and which later became the property of A G Macdonald. Macdonald lent it to the GIFA 1862 (373) having paid the artist that October 'for touching up a picture Glencoe £20' (Account Book). It was seen again the next year at the RSA (319) but is now untraced

50

SUNDOWN — LOCH ACHRAY   1864

oil on canvas[1]

81.3 × 125.7 (32 × 49½)

signed and dated lower right *Horaito.* [sic]
McCulloch. 1864

lent by Glasgow Art Gallery and Museum

Prov: Commissioned by James Patrick by July 1863
and paid for Feb 1864 £262 10s[2]; (his sale
?1869); David Adam Smith; inherited by his
sister Mrs Janet Rodger; her Bequest 1901
Reg No 998

Exh: 1864 Edinburgh RSA (231) *Sundown —
Loch Achray* the property of James Patrick Esq
Benmore Argyleshire

Ref: *Edinburgh Evening Courant* 13 Feb and
10 March 1864; *The Art Journal* 1864 pp 118-20;
Fraser p 32

Loch Achray is situated in the Trossachs between Loch
Katrine and Loch Venachar. Featured in Scott's 'The
Lady of the Lake' (1810) it immediately became an
essential destination for the diligent tourist.

McCulloch however did not exhibit a Loch Achray
subject before 1860, in which year a large oil,
commissioned by Matthew Muir, was shown at the
RSA[3]. McCulloch returned to Loch Achray in the
summer of 1863 to make studies for 'two large pictures'
and whilst he was there received a letter from George
B Simpson, the Dundee collector, regarding the
possibility of purchasing the studies. McCulloch's reply[4]

was non-committal '. . . I cannot say what the price
may be until I finish them and if I succeed in making
them ['them' crossed out] good pictures the price will
be at least as much as my most careful works'. Simpson
was not to acquire the studies. One seems to have been
sold straight away to D R Hay for £52 10s[5], and a
second the following February to Dott for £20. The
latter was probably the working study for this picture,
the former was a small version of Cat No 51 and is
discussed in that entry.

McCulloch's 1863 letter was written on notepaper
headed *The Manse* where presumably he was staying
on this occasion. This view is taken from the northern
shore of the loch only a few minutes walk from the
Manse. The Trossachs Church is visible in the painting
to the right and the massive bulk of Ben Venue
dominates the scene.

1 Canvas stamped 'PREPARED BY/CHARLES ROBERSON/. . .
1 LONG ACRE LONDON'

2 Letter dated July 1863 quoted in this entry, and Account
Book; old label on back of frame (in ink) 'Loch Achray
The property of James Patrick Esq of Kilmun Horatio
McCulloch'

3 (301) *Loch Achray and the Trossachs* the property of
Matthew Muir. Muir paid £250 for it on 7 July 1859
(Account Book). It was exh 1862 London (706) and 1867
Edinburgh Clark Exh (37) *Loch Achray 1859* lent by M M
Muir Esq. It was probably also the GIFA 1861 exhibit (283)
although no owner's name is given in the catalogue

4 Letter to George B Simpson 14 July 1863 (NLS 6350 No
175)

5 Account Book 'July 1863 . . . Mr Hay Princes Street for a
study of Loch Achray £52.10'

LOCH ACHRAY   1865

oil on canvas[1]

80.8 × 125.6 (31½ × 49)

signed and dated lower left centre *H McCulloch 1865*

lent by Glasgow Art Gallery and Museum

Prov: Commissioned by James Patrick by July 1863 and paid for 26 Jan 1865 £262 10s[2]; (his sale ?1869); David Adam Smith; inherited by his sister Mrs Janet Rodger; her Bequest 1901 *Reg No 999* (as *Loch Achray – Morning*)

Exh: 1865 Edinburgh RSA (669) *Loch Achray* lent by James Patrick Esq of Kilmun

Ref: *The Art Journal* 1865 pp 111-13; *Scotsman* 15 Feb 1865; *Edinburgh Evening Courant* 9 March 1865; Fraser p 32

For notes on Loch Achray and McCulloch's visits there see previous entry.

This picture was done from a study made in the summer of 1863 which was immediately sold to D R Hay[3] but presumably retained or borrowed back by the artist to enable him to execute this larger version. This suggestion is supported by the fact thay Hay paid a further £2 10s 'ballance of price of picture Locharay' [sic] on 19 Jan 1865 a week before James Patrick paid for the present painting[4].

The painting has been restored recently and this involved a certain amount of retouching. The reproduction in this catalogue displays a phenomenon known as metamerism which affects the colour values of some retouches when photographed in colour causing apparently mismatched areas, seen here in the hills[5].

1   For technical report see p 103

2   Letter quoted in previous entry and Account Book; framemaker's label of Aitken Dott 14 & 16 South St David Street, Edinburgh

3   See previous entry, note 5. Now untraced, the picture is repr Fraser pl 14

4   D R Hay's *Loch Achray* was exhibited in Glasgow that year at the GIFA (16) and reviewed in the *Glasgow Herald* 18 Feb 1865

5   Metamerism is discussed in detail by Sarah Staniforth in 'Retouching and Colour Matching: The Restorer and Metamerism' *Studies in Conservation* Vol 30 1985 pp 101-11

52

LOCH KATRINE   1866

oil on canvas

110.7 × 182.8 (44 × 72)

signed and dated lower right *H. McCulloch 1866*

lent by Perth Museum and Art Gallery

LOCH KATRINE FROM THE BOATHOUSE 1842

Prov: Purchased from the artist by William Harrison 400 guineas[1]; (?)Joseph Harrison sale Christie's 10 May 1884 lot 71 bt Denison £451 10s; (?)Christie's 15 July 1899 lot 39 bt Longsden £315[2]; (?)Lord Grimthorpe sale Christie's 29 May 1908 lot 451 bt Wallis £99.15s[3]; purchased by Perth Museum and Art Gallery 1937 from J B Bennett & Sons, Glasgow £65   *Reg No 2/132*

Exh: 1866 Edinburgh RSA (453) *Loch Katrine* the property of William Harrison Esq; 1867 Paris *Universal Exhibition* as *Loch Katrine Perthshire* lent by William Harrison; 1960 Paisley Art Gallery; 1966 Milngavie; 1978 Edinburgh NGS *The Discovery of Scotland* (9.14) repr pl viii and fig 105; 1983 London Arts Council (and tour) *Landscape in Britain 1850-1950* (4) repr in colour in catalogue

Ref: *Scotsman* 17 Feb 1866; *The Art Journal* 1866 p 137; James Morrison 'Horatio McCulloch Painter of the Highland landscape' *Seer* June 1980 repr p 17; M Jacobs and M Warner *Art in Scotland* 1980 p 24 repr p 25; Graham Smith 'William Henry Fox Talbot's Views of Loch Katrine' *Bulletin, Museums of Art and Archaeology* The University of Michigan VII 1984-5 p 58 note 44, repr p 71 fig 25

Engraving after J M W Turner 1834

Lithograph after McCulloch 1851

It was impossible for the cultured Victorian to see Loch Katrine without recalling Scott's famous verse:

> One burnish'd sheet of living gold,
> Loch Katrine lay beneath him roll'd,
> In all her length far winding lay,
> With promontory, creek, and bay,
> And islands that, empurpled bright,
> Floated amid the livelier light,
> And mountains, that like giants stand,
> To sentinel enchanted land.
> High on the south, huge Benvenue
> Down on the lake in masses threw
> Crags, knolls and mounds, confusedly hurl'd,
> The fragments of an earlier world;
> A wildering forest feather'd o'er
> His ruin'd sides and summit hoar,
> While on the north, through middle air,
> Ben-an heaved high his forehead bare.'
> 'The Lady of the Lake' Canto 1 XIV

The citizens of Glasgow would also associate this romantic place with modern technology: it was the source of their newly installed piped-water supply, which amazing feat of engineering skill had been opened by the Queen and Prince Albert in 1859.

However McCulloch's young friend the poet Alexander Smith was more impressed by the feats of Sir Walter: 'Scotland is Scott-land. He is the light in which it is seen'. Smith also wrote of this picture 'As a view of Highland scenery we have never seen its equal; and no man but MacCulloch could have produced it' (*Scotsman loc cit*).

McCulloch's earliest recorded Loch Katrine subject was his 1843 RSA exhibit (36) *Loch Katrine, from the Boat House* (see illus). A second (different) view (see

illus) was included in Lawson's *Scotland Delineated* (1847-54) — the original picture was sold to E Gambart & Co[4] who published the lithograph of it on 1 March 1851. Apart from a small 'Loch Katrine' sold to Aidie the Edinburgh dealer along with two other pictures in 1858 (Account Book), McCulloch did not attempt the subject again until the 1860s. Fraser records that the artist spent two months in the autumn of 1861 at Loch Katrine and brought back two studies. One of these would have been the basis for his 1862 RSA exhibit[5] and the second probably the study for the present work[6], which was presumably begun when Harrison made a part payment for it in September 1865. Here the loch is shown from a viewpoint already well-known through Túrner's 1834 illustration to Scott's *Poetical Works* (see illus)

1   Account Book 20 Sept 1865 'Received from Mr Harrison part payment for a picture price four Hundred Guineas £210.' The final payment is not recorded — the last entry in the Account Book was for 24 Nov 1865 'Mr Dott accepted a Bill to be paid to him when I receive the balance of a picture of Loch Katrine, Bill Thirty Pounds. £30'

2   As 'Loch Katrine 1866 41½ × 70'

3   As 'Loch Katrine 1866 43 × 72'

4   Account Book 7 Oct 1850 '. . . from E Gambart Esq for a picture Loch Katherin £45'. Ernest Gambart (1814-1902), art dealer and publisher.

5   (376) *Ben Venue — Loch Katrine, from near the Silver Strand* purchased by Sir Andrew Orr (see Fraser pl 17 and text opposite) Exh again Glasgow GIFA 1862 (72) and Edinburgh 1863 (47)

6   It has not been possible to locate the drawing repr Morrison *op cit* p 15

53

LOCH MAREE ROSS-SHIRE   1866

oil on canvas

111.4 × 183.2 (43$\frac{7}{8}$ × 72$\frac{1}{8}$)

signed and dated lower right *H McCulloch. 1866*

lent by Glasgow Art Gallery and Museum

Prov: Commissioned by David Hutcheson[1] and sold to him by Feb 1867 (see *Exh*); David Adam Smith; inherited by his sister Mrs Janet Rodger; her Bequest 1901   *Reg No 1002*

Exh: 1867 Edinburgh RSA (391) *Loch Maree, Ross-shire* the property of David Hutcheson Esq; 1867 Edinburgh Clark Exh (58) *Loch Maree Ross-shire* lent by David Hutcheson Esq; 1868 Glasgow GIFA (321) *Loch Maree* the property of David Hutchison Esq

Ref: *Edinburgh Evening Courant* 19 Feb 1867; *Glasgow Herald* 4 and 20 Feb 1868; *The Art Journal* 1 May 1868 p 88; Fraser p 32 repr pl 21; Christopher Wood *Dictionary of Victorian Painters* Woodbridge 1971 repr p 321; Irwin p 335

It is not a surprise to discover that Horatio McCulloch sketched Loch Maree from exactly the same spot at which today holiday coach drivers stop to allow their passengers to admire and photograph the scenery. The location is on the A832 about 6 miles from Gairloch, just before the road swings north towards Poolewe. The painting shows the view looking south-west down to Tollie Farm and the landing place in Tollie Bay, and across the water towards the cluster of islands in the centre of Loch Maree. The artist has made some changes to the immediate foreground, and the precipitous rocks bordering the loch and the bare mountain ranges in the middle and far distance, are slightly exaggerated for dramatic effect.

McCulloch's only recorded visit to Ross-shire was in the early autumn of 1859. On 8 September he wrote to Dott from Gairloch Inn[2] requesting financial assistance '. . . unless you can oblige me I will be in a mess as it will take all the cash I have with me to pay my expenses in the Highlands. I have already finished three pictures and am determined to stay if possible until I finish another two. They are all first rate subjects and I can turn them into cash as soon as I have done with them. One of them is Loch Maree the picture you are making the frame for Mr Don . . . I will be home about the first of October.'

The Account Book supports the evidence of this letter: in November 1859 there is a payment from W D Clark for 'a study of Loch Maree Ross shire £40', which was to be the model for the present painting[3]. Clark being an old friend, it was not a problem for McCulloch to borrow back the 1859 study in order to produce the large 1866 version.

A second of the five subjects referred to in the letter to Dott quoted above, was sold in April 1860 to John Don of Broughty Ferry[4], and several other Loch Maree and Ross-shire titles occur, either as exhibits or in the Account Book, in the early 1860s.

As the artist's 'last great effort' *Loch Maree* attracted considerable notice during its 1868 Glasgow showing. Sheriff Bell, in his opening speech to the Institute exhibition, singled it out 'I cannot omit to allude to a picture contributed by our townsman Mr David Hutcheson, the last great effort of our beloved landscape painter MacCulloch, in which he reproduces that finest, perhaps, of all our northern lakes Loch Maree, with all that power and vividness which his pencil could so well command' (*Glasgow Herald* 4 Feb 1868). Whilst the *Art Journal* critic was quite overwhelmed 'From the easel of the lamented Horatio McCulloch, we have besides the 'Lowland River' [Cat No 33] the 'Loch Maree', the very last production, and let us say, as we do advisedly, the very best that ever came from the same gifted hand . . . We acknowledge with chastened feeling the might of a genius that has left no equal in Scotland; nay, rather perhaps we might say, no equal in his own walk of Art in any country in Europe'.

1   According to Fraser in caption to pl 21. There is no record of the price paid nor the exact date of purchase because the last entry in McCulloch's Account Book is for 24 Nov 1865

2   Letter in RSA Library. For a note on Dott see p 106

3   Untraced; 1867, Edinburgh Clark Exh (6) *Loch Maree Rosshire painted on the spot* lent by W D Clark. The entry states that 'Mr Hutcheson's great picture [ie the present picture] was painted from this study'

4   £157 10s (Account Book); (?)1911 Glasgow (195) *Loch Maree* and 1912 Dundee (386) both lent by R B Don

(54-61) The watercolours in this final group are difficult to date precisely, but they almost certainly belong to the last decade of the artist's life.

Common characteristics are the increased use of bodycolour, sometimes enriched by the application of gum, showing that McCulloch was following the course taken by many 19th century artists — that to attract purchasers for works on paper it was necessary to produce bold, richly coloured watercolour paintings which would stand comparison with oils in the exhibition rooms.

Judging from sales recorded in his Account Book McCulloch's output of watercolours increased after about 1860, and many of them were bought by the Edinburgh picture dealers at £2 or £3 each. The two exhibition pieces however (Cat Nos 60, 61), were priced at £26 5s each, an indication that McCulloch's productions for the dealers were less elaborate (and unframed).

54

LANDSCAPE   *c*1860

pencil, watercolour and bodycolour

15×23.2 ($5\frac{7}{8} \times 9\frac{1}{8}$)

signed lower left centre *H McCulloch*

lent from a private collection

Prov: Acquired 'at a sale in Helensburgh' in the late 1940s

55

LANDSCAPE WITH STREAM AND CASTLE   *c*1860

watercolour and bodycolour on cream wove paper

17.7×25.3 ($6\frac{15}{16} \times 9\frac{15}{16}$)

signed lower right *H McCulloch*

lent by Glasgow Art Gallery and Museum

Prov: Thomas D Smellie Bequest 1901   *Reg No 961*

Exh: 1901 Glasgow *International Exhibition* (1063) or (1080) as *Woodland Landscape*

56

LANDSCAPE WITH MOUNTAIN BACKGROUND   *c* 1860

watercolour and bodycolour on cream wove paper

17.8×25.4 (7×10)

signed lower left *H McCulloch* inscribed *verso* (in pencil) *Castle in the Point/of Killearn*

lent by Glasgow Art Gallery and Museum

Prov: Thomas D Smellie Bequest 1901   *Reg No 960*

Exh: 1901 Glasgow *International Exhibition* (1063) or (1080) as *Woodland Landscape*

Despite the inscribed title, the subject has not been identified. There is no castle of this type in the vicinity of Killearn near Glasgow.

NEAR GLENCOE   *c*1860

watercolour heightened with white bodycolour on cream wove paper

16.9 × 24.9 ($6\frac{5}{8}$ × $9\frac{3}{4}$)

signed lower left *H. McCulloch*

lent by The National Galleries of Scotland

Prov: Purchased 1966   *(D4914)*

Ref: Julian Halsby *Scottish Watercolours* London
        1986 pl 43

It has been suggested that the subject is not Glencoe but Appin Bay with Castle Stalker.

57

LANDSCAPE   *c*1860

pen and brown ink, watercolour and bodycolour with some gum on wove paper pasted on card[1]

15.1 × 23.2 ($5\frac{7}{16}$ × $9\frac{1}{8}$)

signed lower left (in ink) *H. McCulloch*

lent from a private collection

Prov: Purchased at a Morrison McChlery & Co sale,
        Glasgow c1959 by present owner

1   *Verso* old label in ink '2474', and in pencil 579D

58

LANDSCAPE   *c*1865

watercolour and bodycolour

18 × 26.1 ($7\frac{1}{8}$ × $10\frac{1}{4}$)

signed lower right *H McCulloch*

lent by The National Galleries of Scotland

Prov: Allan Stark Bequest 1983   *(D5117)*

59

60

IN THE WOOD   *c1865*

watercolour and bodycolour with some gum

23.5 × 35.5 ($9\frac{1}{4}$ × 14)

signed lower right *H McCulloch*

lent by Dundee Art Galleries and Museums (Orchar Collection)

Prov: Presumably purchased by J G Orchar from the 1866 RSA Exh, £26 5s[1]; his Bequest to the burgh of Broughty Ferry 1896   *(179)*

Exh: 1866 Edinburgh RSA (132) *In the Wood*; 1867 Edinburgh Clark Exh (83) lent by J G Orchar; 1888 Glasgow *International Exhibition* (1388) lent by J G Orchar

Ref: *Edinburgh Evening Courant* 26 Feb 1866; *Scotsman* 26 Feb 1866; Julian Halsby *Scottish Watercolours* London 1986 p 112

This and Cat No 61 were probably inspired by McCulloch's visit in 1862 to his old sketching haunt, Cadzow Forest (see entry for Cat No 12). The original Aitken Dott frames[2] and gold mounts have survived. They illustrate how such watercolours were intended to be displayed in the exhibition rooms, where they had to compete with oil paintings hung in close proximity.

1   According to *Edinburgh Evening Courant (loc cit)*

2   Framemaker's label on backing board and back of frame respectively

61

THE EDGE OF A WOOD   *c1865*

watercolour and bodycolour

26.1 × 35.5 ($10\frac{1}{2}$ × 14)

signed lower left *H MCulloch*

lent by Dundee Art Galleries and Museums (Orchar Collection)

Prov: Presumably purchased by J G Orchar from the 1866 RSA Exh; his Bequest to the burgh of Broughty Ferry 1896   *(178)*

Exh: 1866 Edinburgh RSA (3) *The Edge of a Wood*; 1867 Edinburgh Clark Exh (84) lent by J G Orchar; 1888 Glasgow *International Exhibition* (1325) lent by J G Orchar

Ref: *Edinburgh Evening Courant* 26 Feb 1866; *Scotsman* 26 Feb 1866; Julian Halsby *Scottish Watercolours* London 1986 p 112

62 *(Illus p 16)*

Daniel Macnee (1806-82)

HORATIO McCULLOCH   1828

coloured chalks

40.6 × 33 (16 × 13)

signed lower left *D Macnee* dated lower right *1828*

lent by the Scottish National Portrait Gallery

Prov: Presented by T Richardson & Co 1889   *(356)*

In this, the earliest of several portraits of McCulloch by
his friend Daniel Macnee, McCulloch's slightly
dishevelled appearance helps to create a romantic
image of the young artist at the start of his career.

Daniel Macnee (1806-82)

HORATIO McCULLOCH   1842

oil on canvas

91.4 × 71.1 (36 × 28)

inscribed on the artist's sketching board *Horatio
McCulloch/R.S.A./Daniel Macnee/R.S.A*

lent by Glasgow Art Gallery and Museum

Prov: R M Smith by Nov 1874 when he presented the
portrait to the city through Daniel Macnee
Reg No 492

Exh: 1842 Glasgow WSA (50); 1894 Glasgow RGIFA
(301); 1912 London Whitechapel Art Gallery;
1974 Knox Exh (39)

Ref: *Glasgow Courier* 20 Oct 1842; *Lord Provosts of
Glasgow* Glasgow 1883 p 30; Irwin pp 310-11,
pl 176

In this painting Macnee portrays his friend Horatio as a
thoroughly pleasant, fresh-faced young gentleman
gazing eagerly at his subject, nature. In the Hill and
Adamson calotype (see frontis piece), taken only a year
or two later, the slightly scowling expression betrays a
more volatile temperament and his somewhat ravaged
appearance seems to confirm Fraser's hint (p 27) that
McCulloch was inclined to dissipation: 'He started in
life at a time when habits of convivial indulgence were
excessive, and with his generous and open disposition
he could not well in his younger days avoid
participating in its excess'.

63

64 *(Illus p 19)*

Thomas Frank Heaphy (1813-73)

HORATIO McCULLOCH AND W B JOHNSTONE

pen and ink

25 × 13 ($9\frac{7}{8}$ × $6\frac{7}{8}$)

inscribed (above drawing of McCulloch) *Landscape*
and (above drawing of Johnstone) *Religion, Poetry,
and History* lower left *To the Royal Scottish
Academy/this Cartoon of two of the most/
resplendent and meteoric of the/Galaxy of their
Geniuses is most/respectfully dedicated by their/
intensest admirer/T.F.H.*

lent by the Scottish National Portrait Gallery

Prov: Transferred from the National Gallery of
Scotland 1952   *(1783)*

McCulloch's friendship with William Borthwick
Johnstone (1804-68) is described on p 18.
   This drawing was probably done in the 1840s when
both McCulloch and Johnstone had contact with
London artists through exhibitions and visits to the
English capital. However no other record of a link with
Heaphy has been found.

APPENDIX

Works by or ascribed to McCulloch in Glasgow Art Gallery collection but not included in the exhibition

A

Horatio McCulloch

INCHMURRIN – LOCH LOMOND   1849

oil on canvas

91.4 × 156.2 (36 × 61½)

signed *H McCulloch*

Glasgow Art Gallery and Museum

> *Prov:* (?) Purchased from the artist 5 May 1849 by RAPFAS £100[1] and awarded as a prize to James Dyson, Rochdale[2]; David Adam Smith; inherited by his sister Mrs Janet Rodger; her Bequest 1901   *Reg No 1000* (unlocated)
>
> *Exh:* (?)1849 Edinburgh RSA (85) *Scene on the Island of Inch Murran, Loch Lomond*

Ref: (?)*Scotsman* 3 March 1849; *The Art Journal* 1 April 1849 p 101

Despite a discrepancy in the measurements, this was probably McCulloch's 1849 RSA exhibit.

The 1935 Glasgow Art Gallery *Catalogue* describes the picture as follows: 'A woodland scene, to right, two large oak trees, one decayed; to left, deer and sheep'. This agrees with a contemporary description in the *Scotsman* '. . . Two oak trees are the chief objects, one decayed and the other in fresh vigour . . .'

1 '. . . for a Picture size 4 feet 6 in by 3 feet 6 in "Inch Morran Loch Lomond" £100' (Account Book)

2 RAPFAS *Report* for 1849-50

B

Horatio McCulloch

ROSS-SHIRE LANDSCAPE   *c*1860

oil on canvas

30.2 × 45.4 (11⅞ × 17⅞)

signed lower left *H. McCulloch*

Glasgow Art Gallery and Museum

Prov: Thomas D Smellie Bequest 1901   *Reg No 974*

C

Attributed to **Horatio McCulloch**

LOCH LOMOND

oil on paper stuck on canvas

25.4 × 35.5 (10 × 14)

signed lower right *H. McCulloch*

Glasgow Art Gallery and Museum

Prov: Mrs H W Frame Bequest 1985   *Reg No 3407*

Uncertain attribution to **Horatio McCulloch**

BOWLING   (?)1857

oil on canvas

73.5 × 99 (29 × 39)

inscribed lower left *H. McCulloch* [?] *1857*

Glasgow Art Gallery and Museum

Prov: Presented by Mr McIlwraith 1942   *Reg No 2289*

It is difficult to reconcile the unsophisticated handling of the overall design and the clumsy treatment of individual passages of this painting with an attribution to McCulloch. Nevertheless the possibility that it is a very early work to which the signature and date were added later, or that McCulloch had some part in its production, should not be discarded. The following report was contributed by Norma Johnson on completion of recent cleaning and restoration, with reference to pigment analysis carried out by Joyce H Townsend:

    The painting had been previously overcleaned and subsequently heavily overpainted, particularly in the sky, to hide extensive cracking in the paint layer. Pigment analysis indicates a pink ground similar to that used for Cadzow Forest (Cat No 12). The paint itself is untypically thick in the sky and there is some doubt as to its authenticity although it is signed and dated. It is possible that it is an early work, the signature and date having been added (?) by McCulloch at a later stage.

Ascribed to **McCulloch**

LANDSCAPE

oil on panel

30.3 × 45.7 (12 × 18)

inscribed lower left *H McCulloch*

Glasgow Art Gallery and Museum

Prov: Presented by Mrs Inglis Pollock 1953
        Reg No 2996

Unknown (previously attributed to **McCulloch**)

SEAPIECE AND SHIPPING

oil on canvas

19 × 40.6 ($7\frac{1}{2}$ × 16)

inscribed lower right *H McCulloch*

Glasgow Art Gallery and Museum

Prov: Adam Teacher Bequest 1898   *Reg No 775*

The 'signature' has been added

TECHNICAL REPORT

The landscape painter Alexander Fraser included a description of McCulloch's studio technique in his biography of the artist. Fraser's account is of considerable historical interest and also of value for comparison with modern scientific analysis of McCulloch's materials and methods.

'His materials he liked to have about him in great abundance. They were carelessly kept, and in the days of bladders they were generally burst at the first squeeze: in the later days the tubes invariably at once lost their tops[1]. His pallet was always very dirty, but full of colour, − *white* in abundance, and nearest his hand; then *Naples yellow, ochre, raw* and *burnt sienna*; then blue, *French ultramarine; vermilion,* or *Indian red*; then the browns, *bitumen*, and *vandyke*; with a touch of *black* at the extreme end. He used megilp[2] for his earlier pictures; for his later, Robertson's medium, and in great quantities. In his painting-room he wrought standing, with only one brush in his hand at a time. In painting his trees and foreground he used largely − too largely indeed − a goose-quill sable. To this he owed the round touch of which we get too much in his foliage, and also the rather clumsy slanting dash used in his grass and fern painting.

In beginning a picture he rubbed it in thinly, giving at once the effect aimed at − keeping his masses of greys, yellows, and browns very distinct and decided. His works in this state were often very beautiful and suggestive. In the second painting the work was solid, carefully retaining the grey tints. In this state the picture was sometimes somewhat hard and unpromising; but his final painting was always a course of rich glazings, which gave that peculiar brilliancy and richness of colouring so characteristic of his works − varying from tints of extreme delicacy to tones the deepest, mellowest, and most powerful. He was too fond of *Naples yellow* − a colour of extreme beauty, but easily tarnished; he made too much use of bitumen and asphaltum, and was too fond of glazing with *ivory black* − sacrificing too much the future for the present moment, by attempting to give at once, by glazing, a tone and delicacy which ought to have been left to time to give. His work was well finished, in the true sense of the word − not minute in detail, but well considered, and not deficient. His more elaborate and principal pictures promise to stand well. Many of his slighter sketches and early works, in which too free a use has been made of asphaltum, have given way, and become seriously injured by cracking and discolouring.'

The validity of some of Fraser's comments can be judged without the aid of science, for example, the use of bitumen has disfigured several of the works in this exhibition. Technical examination is necessary, however, to confirm the pigments described by Fraser. Eight paintings were available for pigment analysis the results of which appear below.

Other characteristics of his working method were noticed during the course of inspection (and in some cases treatment) of all the Glasgow Art Gallery loans as well as several of those from other collections. A brief summary of these follows the pigment analysis together with a comment on X-ray findings and more detailed reports on two particular paintings.

Pigment Analysis

Paint samples, approximately the size of a grain of sugar, were taken from the edges of each of the eight paintings and consequently are principally from the sky or foreground. (Inner samples are only taken where there is central damage which is to be consolidated.) The specimens were embedded in a synthetic resin and ground down to give a cross section of the various layers. These were examined at 100/200 times magnification in order to elucidate the sequence of layers, and individual pigment particles were identified by optical and electron microscopy, and microchemical analysis.

Summary

Pigment analysis shows consistent technique throughout McCulloch's work except for the occasional use of a coloured ground: the grounds used in both *Cadzow Forest* (Cat No 12) and *Bowling* (Cat No 3) have a pink organic pigment mixed with a lead white in oil. The composition of his palette up to *c*1857 as revealed by this analysis agrees with the description given by Fraser except that vandyke brown and Naples yellow were not found (perhaps because of the restricted areas of the samples). It is interesting to note that in spite of the green pigments available, McCulloch chose to use black and yellow ochre, or other mixtures not involving green pigment, to convey vegetation. Only in the works of his last decade were other pigments detected, terre verte, cobalt or cerulean blue and an unidentified yellow (?Naples). As already noted, many of his paintings are disfigured by the use of bitumen as a brown pigment. Bitumen was widely used by 18th and 19th century artists with the unfortunate effect of shrinkage resulting in 'alligatoring' of the paint film.

PIGMENT ANALYSIS

Cat No	Title	Date	Support	Ground	Sample
3	BOWLING	c1830-5	canvas	The painting has been heavily retouched at the edges and samples were not successful	*i* sky: synthetic ultramarine and lead white?
12	CADZOW FOREST	1834	canvas	lead white and pink organic pigment in oil	*i* sky: synthetic blue pigment and lead white *ii* foreground: 1st layer − brown ochre 　　　　2nd/3rd layers − yellow ochre
13	VIEW FROM THE ROMAN CAMP AT DALZELL *(see also detailed report below)*	1835	canvas	lead white/oil	*i* sky: lead white and an unidentified blue pigment (natural ultramarine?)
20	CADZOW FOREST	c1843	canvas	lead white/oil	*i* sky: vermilion, brown and orange ochre in lead white *ii* sky: synthetic ultramarine and lead white *iii* sky: carbon black and a lake to shade horizon *iv* tree trunk: vermilion, carbon black and lead white *v* foreground: yellow ochre and organic lake
29	THE ENTRANCE TO GLENCOE FROM RANNOCH MOOR	1846	canvas	lead white/oil	*i* foreground: yellow and brown ochre, vermilion, carbon black and lead white
39	DUNSTAFFNAGE CASTLE	1854	canvas	*i* lead white/oil *ii* size layer/(oil?)	*i* sky: synthetic ultramarine and lead white *ii* sky: synthetic ultramarine, lead white and vermilion at horizon *iii* mountains: zinc white and vermilion (painted over the sky layer) *iv* foreground: variations of vermilion, synthetic ultramarine, carbon black, yellow ochre in lead white
43	GLEN AFFRIC	1857	canvas coarse?	lead white/oil	*i* sky: synthetic ultramarine, carbon black and lead white *ii* foreground: brown and yellow ochre and carbon black *iii* foreground vegetation: terre verte (painted over the brown foreground)
51	LOCH ACHRAY	1865	canvas	*i* chalk/oil *ii* lead white/oil	*i* sky: vermilion and cobalt or cerulean blue *ii* foreground: variations of unidentified yellow, brown and yellow ochre, carbon black and white lead

X-rays showed direct paint application and no evidence of preparatory work or alterations on primed canvas[3]. Vigorous brushwork in the foreground is thickly applied. In the sky and mountain areas the brushwork is precisely controlled and thinly applied, the foreground is freer and more expressive. Thick paint, deftly applied, gives solidity to trees, plants and rocks.

McCulloch's regard for nature is visually apparent in the handling of his trees and plants where individual characteristics are easily discernible. As the colours of the Scottish landscape are deep, rich and sombre, it can be assumed that the artist was concerned in portraying an accurate representation of the countryside.

Report on Cat No 13

The painting of the *View from the Roman Camp at Dalzell, near Hamilton 1835* came into the studio for technical examination soon after its acquisition. The varnish was patchy and had yellowed and old oil retouchings were discoloured. The varnish was removed with a suitable solvent[4] and the old retouchings were scraped off with a scalpel. The picture had been previously glue lined because of holes in the original canvas. Both the original and the lining canvas had deteriorated around the edges of the stretcher and were split entirely along the top and left edge. The lining canvas was offering no support at all and it was decided to remove it and the brittle glue from the back of the original canvas[5].

Several McCullochs had been successfully wax/resin lined on earlier occasions and it was therefore decided to use this adhesive again. The painting was lined on a vacuum hot table and when this was completed and the facing had been removed, it was apparent that the wax had stained areas of the sky.

Paint samples and cross sections were taken in order to determine the reasons for this occurrence. The results indicated that the original canvas was unusually fine and that adhesion between canvas and ground was poor. The thin ground layer of lead white was covered by several similar layers (lead white/small amounts of natural ultramarine?/oil) which had been agitated until mixed with the ground. This had resulted in a greater number of air bubbles in the paint structure than would be expected and which consequently made it very porous.

The relining canvas was removed and the painting was relined using a different adhesive[6].

Pigment analysis of John Knox *First Steamboat* c1830[7]

Samples were taken from the edges, and included sky, background colours and foreground. The first impression gained from sampling was that the paint was thicker than is usual, and much thicker than that found in most of McCulloch's paintings. Examination of the sections showed that a red preparative layer is present under most of the painting, and certainly beneath the sky and the background trees. Some samples from the foreground, but not all, included this red, which consists of vermilion and carbon black (two varieties, a coarse and a fine one) mixed with white, which is most likely lead white. The technique of using a red ground on the lighter areas of a composition was quite common in the 18th century and earlier and is not unexpected at the date of this work. However none of the McCullochs examined so far show this feature even though McCulloch is said to have been a pupil of Knox.

The sky has been painted in several layers, which accounts for the thickness of the paint. The unclouded blue sky consisted of the following layers:

yellowed ground	– lead and chalk in oil
red	– vermilion, black (see above para)
lighter blue	– indigo-type pigment in lead white
thin brown layer	– lake varnish?
white/off-white	– lead white?
blue	– indigo-type pigment in lead white oleoresinous varnish

The clouded areas of the sky had an additional white or light blue layer, again with indigo-type pigment, on top of this. The layers are of varying thickness, the top blue layers being the thickest by far, and were probably painted almost at the same time, when the layer beneath was still drying.

The leaves of the tree on the right are painted in a mixture of the indigo and a fine-grained synthetic-looking pigment, rather than a green pigment. The dark greenish black foreground is painted in carbon black and vermilion, with a red layer under one of the samples.

The techniques employed in this painting contrast quite strongly with McCulloch's methods.

Norma Johnson and Joyce H Townsend

---

1 Until collapsible metal tubes were introduced in 1841, artists' oil colours were contained in skin bladders

2 A viscous medium produced by dissolving mastic resin in turpentine, then adding linseed oil. It results in an attractive enamel-like finish which unfortunately becomes brittle and yellow with age

3 Grounds containing white lead are impervious to X-rays and therefore finer details are lost.

4 Acetone and white spirit 1:1

5 The paint surface was protected with several layers of Eltoline tissue and the painting taped down around the edges whilst this work was being carried out

6 Beva (ethylene vinyl acetate)

7 See p 9 and illus p 45

TOPOGRAPHICAL INDEX

FRAMEMAKERS

BONNAR & CARFRAE   **15**
From 1870 house painters, gilders and decorators
(previously Purdie, Bonnar & Carfrae
77 George Street and before that
Bonnar & Carfrae 26 Castle Street)
77 George Street, Edinburgh

AITKEN DOTT   29, 39, 49, 50, 51, 60, 61
1844 (first mention) carver and gilder
12 South St David St, Edinburgh

From 1846 carver and gilder
16 South St David St, Edinburgh

From 1854 carver, gilder and framemaker
16 South St David St, Edinburgh

From 1863 carver, gilder and framemaker
14 & 16 South St David St, Edinburgh

From 1874 carver, gilder and framemaker
26 Castle St, Edinburgh

The firm has continued in business at various addresses
up to the present and is now the Scottish Gallery,
94 George St, Edinburgh
   Of surviving contemporary frames on McCulloch
paintings, a high percentage bear the framemaker's label
of Aitken Dott. The artist's Account Book records a steady
sale of 'small pictures' to Dott in the 1850s and 60s and
that Dott helped McCulloch from time to time with loans
of money (see also letter of 8 Sept 1859 quoted in the
entry for Cat No 53).

JAMES WALKER   **35**
1833 (first mention) carver
83 Broughton St, Edinburgh

1834 carver
29 George St, Edinburgh

1835 carver and gilder
30 George St, Edinburgh

From 1836 carver and gilder
31 George St, Edinburgh

1842 (last mention) carver and gilder
31 George St, Edinburgh

The above information is extracted from Edinburgh *Street
Directories*

PREVIOUS COLLECTIONS AND DONORS

LIST OF ILLUSTRATIONS

CREDITS

LENDERS

Mr Joseph Brand
11

The Duke of Buccleuch and Queensberry, KT
37

Bute Museum
5

Allan Caddy
21

The Clydesdale Bank PLC
44

Dundee Art Galleries and Museums
17, 18, 38, 60, 61

Edinburgh, The National Galleries of Scotland
24, 25, 26, 27, 32, 33, 57, 59

Edinburgh, The Scottish National Portrait Gallery
62, 64

Gateshead, Shipley Art Gallery
(Tyne and Wear Museums Service)
30

Glasgow Art Gallery and Museum
2, 3, 13, 22, 34, 39, 40, 42, 43, 46, 47, 49, 50, 51, 53,
55, 56, 63

Glasgow, Hunterian Art Gallery, University of Glasgow
7, 8, 28

Greenock, McLean Museum and Art Gallery
4

Martyn Gregory
6

James Lees-Milne
12

Charles MacStravick
1

Perth Museum and Art Gallery
23, 52

Private Collections
9, 10, 14, 15, 20, 29, 31, 35, 41, 45, 48, 54, 58

Renfrew District Council
19

Royal Scottish Academy of Music and Drama
16

Professor A J M Sykes
36

William Forrest 1805-89 after McCulloch MY HEARTS IN THE
HIGHLANDS, line engraving in *Illustrated Songs of Robert Burns*
RAPFAS 1861 pl 3.